A Practical Guide to Dewey Decimal Classification

Attribution for DDC text(s):

"This content is taken from the Dewey Decimal Classification system, which is copyrighted by OCLC. All rights are reserved by them, and this content was used with their gracious permission. For more information about Dewey, go to oclc.org/en/dewey.html."

Attribution for WebDewey text(s):

"This content is taken from the WebDewey website, which is copyrighted by OCLC. All rights are reserved by them, and this image was used with their gracious permission. To find out how to access this site, go to dewey.org/webdewey/."

Attribution for OCLC trademarks/service marks:

"DDC®, Dewey®, Dewey Decimal Classification®, OCLC®, and WebDewey® are registered trademarks/service marks of OCLC. All rights are reserved by them."

A Practical Guide to Dewey Decimal Classification

Karen Snow

ROWMAN & LITTLEFIELD
Lanham • Boulder • New York • London

Published by Rowman & Littlefield
An imprint of The Rowman & Littlefield Publishing Group, Inc.
4501 Forbes Boulevard, Suite 200, Lanham, Maryland 20706
www.rowman.com

86-90 Paul Street, London EC2A 4NE

Copyright © 2024 by The Rowman & Littlefield Publishing Group, Inc.

All rights reserved. No part of this book may be reproduced in any form or by any electronic or mechanical means, including information storage and retrieval systems, without written permission from the publisher, except by a reviewer who may quote passages in a review.

British Library Cataloguing in Publication Information Available

Library of Congress Cataloging-in-Publication Data

ISBN 978-1-5381-2719-3 (cloth)
ISBN 978-1-5381-2720-9 (paperback)
ISBN 978-1-5381-2721-6 (electronic)

Contents

Acknowledgments		vii
Preface		ix
1	Dewey Decimal Classification in a Nutshell	1
2	Basic Principles of Classification	13
3	WebDewey: The Online Portal to DDC	21
4	Searching and Browsing in WebDewey	27
5	Using Notes and the Manual	35
6	Number Building in DDC Using a Full or Part of a Number From the Schedules	41
7	Advanced Class Number Building Using Table 1—Part 1—The Basics of Adding Standard Subdivisions	49
8	Advanced Class Number Building Using Table 1—Part 2—Approximating the Whole, Groups of People, Biography, and Historical Periods	59

9	Advanced Class Number Building—Including Geographic Places Using Table 2	73
10	Advanced Class Number Building Using Table 3—Subdivisions for the Arts, for Individual Literatures, for Specific Literary Forms	85
11	Advanced Class Number Building Using Tables 4–6—Languages and Ethnic and National Groups	103
12	Conclusion and DDC Resources	115
Appendix A: Answers to End-of-Chapter Exercises		119
Appendix B: Flow Chart for Works By or About More Than One Author		137
Glossary		139
Index		141
About the Author		143

Acknowledgments

A book is never the product of a single mind, and this one is no exception. Though my vision has remained steady through three "Practical Guides," I have had much support that has shaped the content of the books. Tim Butzen-Cahill has been my main cheerleader since I started this book-writing journey; his positive encouragement and feedback have sustained me through the writing process and made all three books so much better. I can't tell you enough how much I appreciate your friendship and support!

Lauren Enjeti continues to delight readers of my books and me through her marvelous illustrations. Thank you for putting up with my strange requests and continuing this journey with me, my glowing friend!

Miriam Rosen and Katie Steffenson also provided excellent and extremely appreciated feedback on the various book drafts. Thank you for your help!

Special thanks and acknowledgment to OCLC for their support of the Dewey Decimal Classification system, WebDewey, and their associated products and services.

Robby and Eleanor—my loves. Thank you for filling my life with so much joy. xoxo.

This book is dedicated to my father, Robert Snow, who gave me so much love and support and always encouraged me to follow my passions, no matter how incomprehensible they were to him. I miss you so much.

Preface

In 1873, an Amherst College undergraduate student had a "Eureka!" moment during a lengthy sermon by the college president. He worked as an assistant at the library and had been reading a number of works about classification systems—in his opinion, none seemed to be a good, practical fit for organizing growing library collections.[1] Though others had previously mentioned the possibility of using decimals in classification, it wasn't until that student, Melvil Dewey, ran with the idea that what is now commonly known as the "Dewey Decimal System" was born. It is now one of the most popular library classification schemes in the world.

In this book, I will refer to Dewey's creation using its official name: Dewey Decimal Classification, or DDC for short, according to the Online Computer Library Center (OCLC), the holder of its copyright. Dewey eventually published the DDC in 1876 (anonymously), and though his classification system is ubiquitous today, it was truly revolutionary at the time. Prior to the release of DDC, most libraries used what is called a *fixed location system* to organize their collections. Fixed location systems rely heavily upon the physical position of a resource in a library for location purposes. For example, a book may be assigned some sort of an identification number based upon the bookcase, shelf, and position on the shelf it can be found within a broad subject area (e.g., History, Bookcase 5, Shelf 3, Book 10).

The fixed location system is fine if it is used for small collections, closed stacks, and/or remote storage facilities that are off-limits to the public and need to preserve space. However, it is problematic for growing collections meant to be browsed by the public. As library collections grew throughout the nineteenth century, this fixed location system became increasingly onerous and impractical. Existing resources were shifted around to make room for new resources, vacating the physical locations they once occupied. Frequent reclassification was necessary.

Melvil Dewey, in an effort to help solve the issues presented by the fixed location system, created a *relative location system*. A relative location system does not take into account the physical location of a resource. Instead, "an information resource will be or might be in a different place each time it is reshelved; that is, it is reshelved relative to what else has been acquired, taken out, returned, and so forth, while it was out for use."[2] A **call number**, of which the classification number is a part, is assigned to each resource to provide its "address" in relation to other resources that have the same or a similar topic. This call number can be used in any library collection—it is not dependent on the exact physical location of the resource itself. In fact, a resource does not need to be in a physical location at all to have a call number; digital resources benefit from having call numbers assigned to them as classification numbers also provide intellectual access—bringing together resources that share the same or similar topics, whether you are browsing the library shelves or the online catalog. Both Dewey Decimal and Library of Congress Classification are relative location systems that provide easier physical and intellectual access to resources.

DDC has been revised and published continuously since 1876 and is currently in its twenty-third edition. It is no longer published regularly in print but can be accessed online using a subscription-based program called WebDewey, which I will refer to throughout this text, or by purchasing DDC in print-on-demand volumes.

This book is part of my passion project to make library cataloging standards more accessible to students, practitioners, and anyone else who is simply interested in the topic. For this reason, just as I did with my previous two books, *A Practical Guide to Library of Congress Classification* and *A Practical Guide to Library of Congress Subject Headings*, I have written a text that focuses more on the practical aspects of finding and constructing DDC numbers and less on the history and philosophical underpinnings of the system. If you are interested in the latter, I highly recommend reading the books listed in the resource list in Chapter 12 of this text. However, that does not mean I won't discuss *any* history and theory. Knowing basic principles of classification (Chapter 2), for example, will help you make better decisions when assigning DDC numbers.

Also, I will not advocate for or against the use of Dewey Decimal Classification in this text. There are many who choose to use other categorization systems or de-emphasize DDC in their library for a variety of reasons, such as their belief that other systems better fit the needs of their users. Moreover, there are ethical issues to consider with DDC, as with any organizational system, such as DDC's emphasis on Western, white, male, Protestant Christian, heterosexual, and cisgender perspectives, and its creator's racist, sexist, and anti-Semitic beliefs and actions. Recently, Melvil Dewey's name was removed from one of the American Library Association's most prestigious awards because of the aforementioned beliefs and actions.[3]

Instead, I will focus more on the *what* and *how* of the classification scheme for those interested in learning more about how DDC works in order to complete schoolwork, assign a class number for your job, or satisfy your curiosity. However, I recommend exploring Dewey's background and ethical considerations in cataloging and classification so you can make more informed choices and have a more holistic understanding of DDC.

In this book, I start by explaining DDC "in a nutshell" and some basic principles of classification so we can lay a theoretical foundation for the class number finding and building to come. Next, I present the main portal for accessing the most current editions of DDC: WebDewey. I will discuss strategies for searching and browsing DDC, as well as the significance of notes and what is called "The Manual" in Chapters 4 and 5.

Then I will discuss an important feature of DDC: class number building. Chapter 6 covers DDC number building within the schedule text, and then Chapters 7–11 explore the basics of number building using Tables 1–6, which provide notation for expressing a wide variety of formats and topics to make a class number more specific (for example, to include in the DDC number that the resource you are classifying is an encyclopedia). The final chapter will provide a conclusion and additional resources to help you build on your DDC knowledge.

Most of the chapters in this book contain exercises at the end that will reinforce the concepts discussed in a specific chapter. I recommend completing these exercises and checking your answers against the ones presented in Appendix A so you can assess your understanding of the topics covered.

I hope that this book will help you gain a better understanding of DDC and how to use it effectively to assign class numbers to organize a library collection. I also hope you will gain an appreciation for classification, which can be simultaneously fascinating and challenging. After all, the initial motto of DDC was "To classify is itself an education."[4] Ready to get started? I hope so! On to learning about DDC "in a nutshell."

NOTES

1. From Dewey, M. (1920, Feb. 15). Decimal Classification beginnings. *Library Journal 45*, p. 152.

2. Joudrey, D. N., and Taylor, A. G. (2018). *The Organization of Information*. Fourth edition. Libraries Unlimited, p. 561.

3. For more information about this aspect of Dewey's legacy, I recommend reading Wayne A. Wiegand's excellent and thorough book *Irrepressible Reformer: A Biography of Melvil Dewey*, published by the American Library Association in 1996, and the article "Melvil Dewey's Name Stripped from Top Library Award," by Brigit Katz, published on June 28, 2019, https://www.smithsonianmag.com/smart-news/melvil-deweys-name-stripped-top-library-award-180972514.

4. Comaromi, J. P. (1976). *The Eighteen Editions of the Dewey Decimal Classification*. Albany, NY: Forest Press, p. 60.

1

Dewey Decimal Classification in a Nutshell

Dewey Decimal Classification (DDC) is an organization system that does double duty—it is meant to both categorize and provide a way to locate a resource within a library collection. Topics are assigned a number that is at least three digits long and represents a class, division, and subdivisions. This number, along with numbers from associated DDC tables, are called **notation**. Notation within DDC will always contain only Arabic numbers (and possibly a decimal point as well); for instance, 419.7 is the DDC number representing American Sign Language, and therefore should be assigned to works that are generally about that topic. Other classification systems have notations that contain letters, numbers, symbols, or combinations of the above. For example, the notation of the Library of Congress Classification, the other major classification system used in the United States, will always contain a letter/number combination, and possibly a decimal as well, such as E159.5 (United States antiquities) and D1159 (Small paintings).

It is also important to note that DDC is organized by discipline, not by subject. For example, the topic "flowers" is not represented by a single classification number. Instead, you are expected to choose a classification number for flowers within the discipline of the resource. Classifying a book about flowers generally? Use the 500 (Science) class. Flower gardening? The 600 (Technology) class. Flower arrangement? The 700 (Arts & Recreation) class. Flowers as a clothing accessory? The 300 (Social

Figure 1.1. Flowers. *Source*: Lauren Enjeti

Sciences) class. I will talk more about this idea later, but in the meantime, let's look at the overall structure of DDC.

STRUCTURE OF DDC

DDC is organized hierarchically into ten main classes, ten divisions within those classes, and ten sections within the divisions. Since there are too many divisions and sections to comfortably list here,[1] I will provide only the ten main DDC classes:

000, Computer Science, Information, General Works
100, Philosophy and Psychology
200, Religion
300, Social Sciences

400, Language
500, Science (including Mathematics)
600, Technology
700, Arts & Recreation
800, Literature
900, History & Geography

Let's dig a little deeper into each of these main classes.

- The **000** class has historically been the place for "Generalia"—general works and miscellaneous topics that do not fit comfortably in the other classes. In fact, Melvil Dewey did not even name this class in the first edition. It includes works that cover multiple disciplines, such as encyclopedias and periodicals. Library and information science, computer science, and journalism are included in this class as well. According to DDC scholar John Comaromi, the reason for putting library and information science in the first main class was obvious to Dewey—since the purpose of DDC is to organize a library collection, *of course* works about libraries should be classed before all other topics.[2]
- The **100** class contains philosophy and psychology, as well as parapsychology and occultism. Philosophy constitutes most of this class, which includes metaphysics, epistemology, ethics, logic, and specific class numbers for philosophical schools. Psychology topics are all tucked into the 150s. The arrangement of philosophy and psychology together in one class is likely a residual of the late nineteenth century thinking in which DDC was created, when the boundaries of the psychology discipline were not clearly defined and philosophy's boundaries were still very permeable.
- The **200** class covers religion, though categories focus primarily on topics related to Christianity, covered in classes 230 through 280. All the other world religions, such as Judaism, Islam, and Buddhism, can be found only in 290 through 299. Dewey's decision to focus on Christianity is likely due to his desire to emphasize primarily American religious experiences and the topics of religious books commonly found in American library collections, which at that time were largely Christian-focused.

- The **300** class, initially labeled by Melvil Dewey as Sociology, covers a wide range of topics under the umbrella of *Social Sciences*. This includes topics in the disciplines of sociology and anthropology, but also collections of general statistics, political science, economics, law, military science, education, transportation, customs, etiquette, and folklore. Yikes! It is no wonder that the 300 class is one of the most crowded of the classes. The inclusion of so many topics also results in the close shelf proximity of seemingly very disparate works, such as books on the study of measurement next to books on costumes. This crowding has led some to argue that the 300 class is a "strange and badly conceived class . . . [that] is the resting ground for the misfits that do not belong in other classes and have some sort of relationship to society, thus creating this strange mélange of topics that are merged together like adopted children in a comfortable home of disparate members."[3]
- The **400** class contains topics related to the study of languages and linguistics, with most of the class numbers devoted to Western languages (English, German, French, Italian, Spanish, Portuguese, Latin, and Greek). This class does not include works of literature, which are placed in the 800 class. Language dictionaries are popular resources classed here.
- The **500** class—called *Natural Science* by Melvil Dewey, but it is now titled just *Science*—is for the "hard science" disciplines, such as mathematics, astronomy, physics, biology, paleontology, botany, and zoology. The order of the 500 class is thought to be inspired by Alexander Bain's order of the sciences in his influential nineteenth century book *Logic*, starting with the more abstract science of mathematics and moving into the more "concrete" sciences the deeper one goes into the 500s.[4]
- The **600** class covers *Technology* (also called the *Applied Sciences*), which includes a wide array of topics such as engineering, medicine, and manufacturing. This class was originally titled the *Useful Arts*, which helps explain why home and family management, office services, and animal husbandry are included in the 600 class as well. Dewey viewed the useful arts as "the result of the application of the laws of nature to man's use," so logically this class should follow the 500 sciences class.[5]

- The **700** class covers what Dewey called the *Fine Arts* (to distinguish it from the *Useful Arts* of the 600 class) but is now called *Arts & Recreation*. It contains architecture, landscape architecture, sculpture, painting, graphic arts, printmaking, photography, and music. The "recreation" part of the title of this class is lumped together interestingly with "performing arts" in the 790s, which also includes sports. Also interestingly, Dewey called the topics of the 790s "Amusements" in the initial editions of DDC.
- The **800** class contains literature and rhetoric, primarily organized by the language of the literature (the same languages of the 400 class). Within each language, you can specify if the work is poetry, drama, fiction, essays, speeches, letters, humor, and satire, or "miscellaneous." DDC accommodates organizing literature by popular genres, such as mystery, romance, science fiction, etc., but only for works by or about *more than one author*. Therefore, quite a few libraries do not use the 800 class to organize their fiction books, using the 800s primarily for classifying poetry, drama, essays, speeches, and letters.
- The **900** class is devoted to history and geography topics, including travel and the history of extraterrestrial worlds! However, most of the class focuses on history, organized primarily by continent—Europe, Asia, North America, South America, and Africa—and then chronologically by events within each geographic area. Australia is placed in the 990 "other areas" alongside Pacific and Atlantic Ocean islands, as well as the Arctic islands and Antarctica.

EXPRESSIVENESS AND HIERARCHY

Now that you have a better sense of the disciplines and topics included in DDC, let's look more closely at the notation itself. The DDC is a **hierarchical classification system**, in which broader topics are subdivided into narrower topics within a specific category. The broad topic of *Science*, for instance, can be subdivided by *Mathematics*, which can be further subdivided by *Algebra, Arithmetic, Geometry*, and so on.

In addition, the DDC has a very "expressive" notation. If a classification system has **expressive** notation, that means that the notation itself communicates the hierarchical relationships of the topic it represents. To give you a better idea of what expressive, hierarchical notation looks like, let's explore how DDC numbers can be broken down by class, division, and section.

The DDC **main class** is represented by the first digit in a class number. For example, the number "6" of 6̲00 represents *Technology*.

The DDC **division** is represented using the second digit in a class number. For example, the number "1" of 61̲0 represents *Medicine and Health* within *Technology*.

The DDC **section** is represented by the third digit. 616̲. For example, the second "6" represents *Diseases*, within *Medicine and Health* (61̲0), within *Technology* (6̲00).

Each digit within 616 expresses a different layer of the topic's hierarchy, as shown in Figure 1.2.

LENGTH OF DDC NUMBERS

The DDC number will always be at least three digits long, with the option of adding a decimal point between the third and fourth digit and further notation for more specific topics within a DDC section. For example, *Diseases of the digestive system* is represented by the number "3" (within the broader categories of *Diseases*) after the decimal point in 616.3̲. The length of the DDC number depends on the specificity of the topic, as well

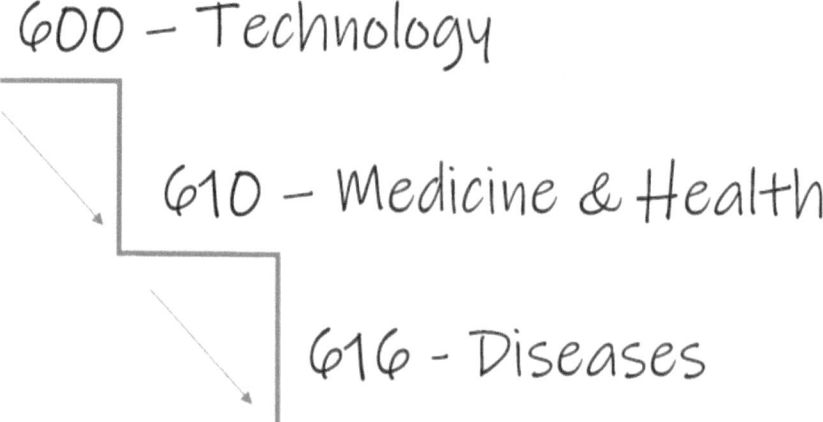

Figure 1.2. Hierarchy of 616. *Source*: Karen Snow

as the needs of the library—the longer the number, the more difficult it is to fit it on a book's spine label!

As we'll see when we explore the DDC tables in Chapters 7–11, we can build class numbers that include attributes such as the format of the resource (e.g., dictionary, periodical), time period (e.g., twentieth century, 1950s), and geographic location (e.g., United States, Pacific Ocean). With the addition of these table notations (which are not required, by the way), as well as other notation that can be added through other types of number building, DDC numbers can get lengthy. Take a look at the breakdown of the DDC number representing the topic "ambulance services in Germany" in Figure 1.3.

If there is little need to include the geographic aspect in 362.1880943 (and you don't want the spine label to wrap around the book!), then you may decide to exclude the Table 1 notation (--09) and Germany from Table 2 (--43), and use only 362.188 (ambulance services), which should be sufficient if you have very few resources in your collection on this topic.

But let's go back to the decimal point for a moment. The introduction to DDC notes that "The dot is not a decimal point in the mathematical sense, but a psychological pause to break the monotony of numerical digits and to ease the transcription and copying of the class number."[6] Some libraries have policies stating that DDC numbers can be only certain lengths; for example, do not assign DDC numbers that have more than two, three, or four numbers to the right of the decimal point.

Having a blanket policy is problematic as you must be very careful about where to remove numbers in case you accidentally create nonsensical DDC numbers. For example, 796.8309 represents the history of boxing. If my institution has a policy of "no more than three digits past the

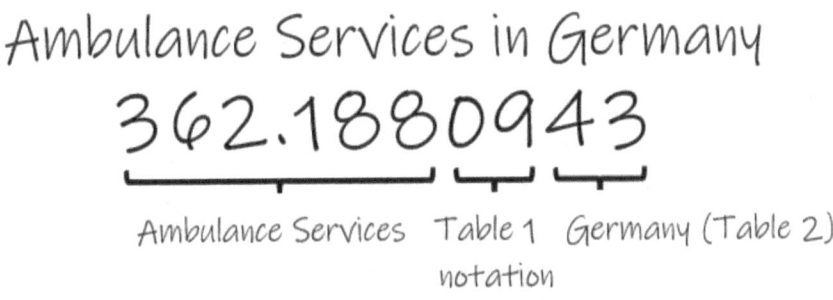

Figure 1.3. Ambulance Services in Germany. *Source:* Karen Snow

decimal point," then I would have to exclude the final "9." The resulting class number, 796.830, is meaningless in the context of DDC. Not only should a DDC number with a decimal point never have a zero at the end, but the "0" in the example class number is a required part of the Table 1 notation --09 (history) and has no meaning on its own. Therefore, if you need to shorten 796.8309, it is best to shorten it to 796.83 (boxing). This is why understanding how DDC numbers are built will serve you well if you work with DDC in any capacity. Good thing we cover number building in later chapters of this book!

QUICK TIP . . .

Never end a DDC number with a zero if the notation includes a decimal point. Also, even though many libraries have policies regarding the length of DDC numbers, such policies may produce incorrect class numbers if one is not mindful of the meaning of each part of the class number.

FEATURES OF DDC

DDC is organized by class numbers within what are called **schedules** that list the notations, captions, and instructions for the class numbers. Once again, notation consists of characters that represent a class, division, and subdivisions (for example, 616) or topics within tables (for example, --09), but the **caption** (also called a **heading**) presents the specific meaning of the notation in English words (for example, "Diseases" is the caption for the class number 616).

As a reminder, DDC is ordered according to disciplines or fields of study and not necessarily by subject matter. For example, books on toys will be found in different classification numbers based upon the focus of the book: the making of toys is represented by 688.72, playing with toys can be found at 790.133, toy safety at 363.19, and the cataloging of toys at 025.3496. The DDC **Relative Index** is a handy tool that brings together all locations of a subject under one entry. It is an index that lists subjects alphabetically and then alphabetically by discipline within each subject. I will talk more about the Relative Index in Chapter 3.

DDC is updated on a regular basis by the Dewey editorial office located at the Library of Congress, where it has been since the 1920s. It is available in both unabridged and abridged versions. The abridged version is geared toward smaller library collections (about twenty thousand volumes or less) that do not need the level of specificity necessary in larger collections.

WHERE CAN I FIND DDC?

In 2017, the DDC editorial office announced it will no longer regularly publish a print version of DDC. DDC, both abridged and unabridged versions, is now primarily accessible online via **WebDewey**. It is a subscription-based tool that provides access to not only the DDC schedules and tables, but also to other DDC resources, so if you or your affiliated institution do not subscribe to WebDewey, OCLC (the publisher of DDC) does offer a free thirty-day trial. A link to the sign-up form on the web is available in Chapter 12 of this book.

OCLC also offers a "print-on-demand" option for those with unreliable internet access, who lack the funding for the annual subscription, or would simply like to have a print copy. A link for requesting a print copy is provided in Chapter 12 as well. Since WebDewey is currently the primary portal to DDC, that is what I will use to demonstrate searching and browsing DDC in this book. For those of you who likely will not have access to WebDewey after the thirty-day free trial, there are freely available resources, such as LibraryThing, that can help steer you in the right direction when seeking a DDC number. We will discuss these further in Chapter 12.

Finally, after all we've covered in this chapter, you may still be wondering about the letters or letter/number combinations that you see on a spine label *following* the DDC number, like the VAN and Sch525 codes in the Figure 1.4 examples.

What you see after the class number is called by various names—Cutter numbers (named in honor of their creator, Charles Cutter), book numbers, or author numbers are the most common—and are useful for keeping a collection organized primarily by author within a topic on the shelf. For books, most often they are formed from the first-listed author's last name, either by taking the first letters directly from the

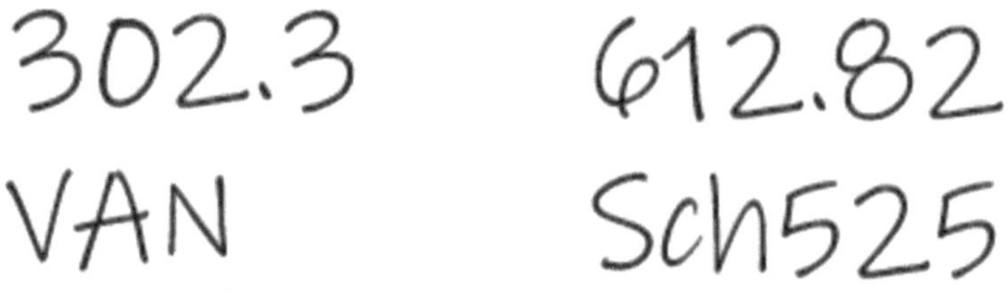

302.3   612.82
VAN   Sch525

Figure 1.4. Examples of Classification & Cutter Numbers. *Source*: Karen Snow

last name (VAN from the name Van Der Linden) or using a table that converts certain letters into numbers (Sch525 representing Schmidt). If your library uses the latter, OCLC offers a free download (for Windows computers) of its Dewey Cutter Program that magically creates Cutter numbers using the Cutter Four-Figure Table or the Cutter-Sanborn Four-Figure Table. You can download it from here: https://help.oclc.org/Metadata_Services/WebDewey/Dewey_Cutter_Program.

Because of the variation in local practices in creating Cutter numbers, I will focus solely on DDC numbers in this book.

Before we look more closely at DDC numbers and how to find and construct them, we should first lay a foundation that will serve us well throughout our journey. There are basic principles of classification discussed in the introduction to Dewey Decimal Classification that will help you make decisions about where best to place a resource in DDC and which number to choose when faced with multiple options. Once you have completed the end-of-chapter exercises for Chapter 1, we will get a little "thinky" about classification in Chapter 2!

CHAPTER 1 EXERCISES

Answer the following questions using the information provided in this chapter. You should not have to search any other source for the answer. Compare your answers to the answers provided in Appendix A.

1. What two things does DDC allow us to do with library collections?
2. In which DDC class do we assign works on library science?
3. Which class number was originally titled the "Useful Arts"?

4. True or False—The index to DDC is called Melvil's Awesome Index.
5. What does it mean to say that a classification system is "expressive"? Provide an example that shows expressive notation.
6. In the DDC number 306, which number represents the DDC . . .
   Section?
   Main Class?
   Division?
7. True or False—DDC numbers will always be at least three digits long.
8. Who publishes DDC? Is DDC still published in print?
9. In the DDC schedules, what do we call the term that provides the specific meaning of a notation?
10. True or False—A DDC number with a decimal point can end with a zero.

NOTES

1. See the DDC Summaries for a full listing of the DDC classes, divisions, and sections: https://www.oclc.org/content/dam/oclc/dewey/resources/summaries/deweysummaries.pdf.
2. Comaromi, *The Eighteen Editions of the Dewey Decimal Classification*.
3. Scott, M. L. (1998). *Dewey Decimal Classification, 21st edition: A Study Manual and Number Building Guide.* Libraries Unlimited, p. 89.
4. Comaromi, *The Eighteen Editions of the Dewey Decimal Classification*.
5. Comaromi, *The Eighteen Editions of the Dewey Decimal Classification*.
6. OCLC. (2019, May 17). *Introduction to the Dewey Decimal Classification.* https://www.oclc.org/content/dam/oclc/dewey/versions/print/intro.pdf (p. 4).

2

Basic Principles of Classification

I highly recommend reading the introduction to Dewey Decimal Classification[1] as it contains a nice overview of DDC's history and structure. It also discusses basic principles of classification that I will summarize here, and I will also provide exercises at the end of the chapter that will test your understanding of how to apply these principles. The basic principles of classification come in handy for many reasons but are particularly important when you are tasked to assign a class number to a resource and you are not certain where to begin. If it helps, try using the following as a checklist to get you started.

WHAT IS THE SUBJECT?

After discussing the principle of hierarchy in the DDC introduction,[2] the DDC editors delve into how to approach the choice of classification number for a resource. They note, "Classifying a work properly depends first upon **determining the subject** of the work in hand."[3] (Quick note: this does not apply to literary works, which I will address shortly). At first glance, this may seem like an obvious and almost silly instruction—*of course* I have to know what this book is about before I can assign a DDC number! For some resources it is quite easy to determine the subject just by looking at the title. The title of this book, *A Practical Guide to Dewey Decimal Classification*, makes it clear that it is about DDC, so no need to stress over choosing the DDC number representing Dewey Decimal Classification (so meta!).

However, determining the subject is often not as easy as it first appears. The reasons for this are manifold: What if the title and other text on the item do not clearly state what the work is about? What if there *is* no text on the item? Or what if the item covers many topics?

Let's say I have to assign a class number to a book titled *Eight Little Piggies* by Stephen Jay Gould. After looking closer at the book, I notice that it is not about piggies (much less eight little ones) but contains the author's reflections on natural history. This example demonstrates that a work's title, if there is one, can be deceptive, and therefore it is important to look elsewhere on and within the item to find information about a work's subject. These places include (keeping in mind that not all items have the following):

- dust jacket,
- back cover,
- table of contents,
- cataloging-in-publication (CIP) data on the back side of the title page,
- bibliographical references,
- container, or
- documentation that came with the main item, like a DVD insert.

In absence of, or in addition to, the above sources, you can also read the contents of the item itself, such as the introduction, preface, and author biography, and consult outside sources, such as the publisher's website or online retailers.

Within DDC, literary works are an exception to the rule of determining the subject as the first step. We classify literary works, such as fiction, poetry, essays, and drama in the literature class (800). Literary works by one author are organized by the language, form, and period in which the work was written. For example, *Pride and Prejudice* and *Sense and Sensibility*, both novels by English author Jane Austen, are classed at the same number (823.7) that captures the fact that both books are novels (form), in English (language), and written during 1800–1837 (time period). No subject matter to be found here! I will provide more information about classifying literary works in Chapter 10 when I discuss Table 3.

WHAT IS THE AUTHOR'S INTENT?

The next question you should ask yourself is, **"What is the author's intent?"** Sometimes this is clear from looking at the information sources listed on page 14, but not always. You will need to ask yourself where the author would want this work placed in a classification system. A book of pig illustrations may serve as a tool for identifying pig breeds, but it may also be a how-to book on how to draw pigs! (see Figure 2.1). The book would be classified in very different class numbers, depending on the intent of the author.

Figure 2.1. *How to Draw Piggies! Source*: Lauren Enjeti

WHAT IS THE DISCIPLINE?

Then, assuming you can determine that the work in hand is about one main subject, then you must **determine the discipline** to which the subject belongs. Since DDC is ordered according to disciplines or fields of study, subjects will be placed in different areas of DDC based upon how the work approaches it. For example, actual works on *pigs* (of which *Eight Little Piggies* is not one) may be placed in multiple areas of the 600 (*Technology*) class, depending on if the work focuses on the care, cultivation, and breeding of pigs (636.4); using them in medical experiments (616.0273); or as agricultural pests (632.69633). The Relative Index is an important resource that can be very helpful for linking subjects to disciplines in DDC, so I recommend consulting it frequently when searching for a particular topic. I will discuss the Relative Index further in Chapter 3.

WHAT IF THE WORK IS ABOUT MULTIPLE SUBJECTS?

What if the work you have in hand is about two or more main subjects? For example, a work that spends equal time discussing pigs and horses?

Or a work that covers pigs, horses, cows, and sheep? Here are the main rules of thumb when confronted with works on multiple subjects:

Rule of Application

The rule that rules them all is the *rule of application*, so if this rule applies, then you can disregard the others. In essence, if you have a work on multiple subjects and one of the subjects is being acted upon by the other subject, then **class the work with the subject that is being acted upon.** To illustrate this, the DDC introduction provides an example of a work that is about William Shakespeare's influence on the poet John Keats. In this example, we should class the work in the class number associated with Keats rather than Shakespeare because the focus of the work is Shakespeare's influence *upon* Keats. Another example is a work on the effect of inflation upon the job market; assign a class number associated with the "job market" and not "inflation" because the job market is the topic being acted upon in this case.

Fuller Treatment

If a work is about two subjects, like in the pigs and horses example, **choose the class number for the subject that receives fuller treatment.** If the author spends approximately 60 percent of the text on pigs and approximately 40 percent on horses, assign to the work the class number for pigs.

First-of-Two Rule

If a work is about two subjects, but both subjects receive equal treatment (and are not used to introduce or explain one another), the first-of-two rule applies. Choose **whichever subject comes first in the DDC schedules.** For example, if the work you are cataloging is about the husbandry of pigs and horses equally, you should choose the class number for horses (636.1) for the work because it comes before the class number for pigs (636.4, swine) in the schedules (the 636.1 through 636.8 range is represented on page 17).

636.1 Horses
636.2 Cattle and related animals
636.3 Sheep and goats
636.4 Swine
636.5 Chickens and other kinds of domestic birds
636.6 Birds other than poultry
636.7 Dogs
636.8 Cats

There are going to be some exceptions to this rule, so pay close attention to special instructions that appear in the schedules!

Rule of Three

If a work is about three or more subjects that are discussed equally, and they are all subdivisions of a broader subject, **class the work in the first higher number that includes all the subjects**. Sticking with the animal husbandry theme, if the work you are cataloging is equally about pigs (636.4), horses (636.1), cows (636.2), and sheep (636.3), you should class that work in animal husbandry (636) because it is the first higher number that includes all those subjects.

Rule of Zero

If a work can be classed in multiple subjects that seem reasonable, **choose the class number with a subdivision beginning with numbers 1–9 rather than 0**. In other words, if you look to the right of the decimal point, the fewer zeros, the better, particularly in the fourth digit. The DDC introduction uses an example of a biography of an American Methodist missionary in China. This work should be classed in 266 (*Missions*) but can technically and correctly be placed in different, yet more specific class numbers within 266:

- 266.0092 (biography of a missionary),
- 266.02373051 (foreign missions of the United States in China), and
- 266.76092 (biography of a United States Methodist Church missionary).

However, using the *rule of zero*, we should choose the last option (266.76092) because the fourth digit is not a zero and there are fewer zeros.

Table of Last Resort

The table of last resort sounds more ominous than it really is. **The purpose of this table (replicated below) is to help a classifier decide on a class number when several class numbers seem to work equally well and the other rules are not helpful.** The table categorizes DDC topics and places them in order of preference (the first category should take precedence over the fifth category, for example). The table of preference is ordered in such a way so that concrete things are preferred over abstract ideas when choosing one DDC number over another.

1. Kinds of things
2. Parts of things
3. Materials from which things, kinds, or parts are made
4. Properties of things, kinds, parts, or materials
5. Processes within things, kinds, parts, or materials
6. Operations upon things, kinds, parts, or materials
7. Instrumentalities for performing such operations

The introduction to DDC provides the example of border patrol surveillance, which one could class in either 363.285 (Border patrols) or 363.232 (Patrol and surveillance). According to the table of last resort, we should choose 363.285 (Border patrols) because "border patrols are a kind of police service" (#1, kinds of things in the table of last resort) as opposed to "patrol and surveillance," which are "processes performed by police services" (#5, processes within things, kinds, parts, or materials in the table of last resort). One word of caution though: if the author of the work emphasizes a concept farther down the table of preference over a thing higher up in the table, then go with the author's preference.

Interdisciplinary Works

If you have a work that covers multiple disciplines (not subjects), then, using the "fuller treatment" rule you should class the work in the discipline that receives fuller treatment. For works that discuss multiple disciplines that receive equal treatment, there are several options. You could use an *interdisciplinary number* provided in DDC for works on one subject that is discussed from different disciplinary angles. You could also explore the use of the generalities class (000) for interdisciplinary works.

Of course, there will always be exceptions. Pay close attention to the Notes area for each class number in case there are instructions specific to that class number. These may come in the form of tables of preference or preference notes. I discuss Notes in more detail in Chapter 5, but as one example, DDC 395—Etiquette (Manners) includes in its Notes area the instruction "Unless other instructions are given, class a subject with aspects in two or more subdivisions of 395 in the number coming last, for example, table manners for children 395.54 (not 395.122)."

If you still feel unsure about where to class a resource, always keep in mind this overarching goal: assign the class number that you think will make the most sense to your users, even if you do not follow DDC instructions to the letter. I promise, there are no Dewey police who will arrest you for doing things a little differently! Also, I recommend finding where other works on that topic (or similar topics) have been classed. Even if you diverge somewhat from the DDC instructions, if the resource fits logically on the shelf with others of a similar topic, that should still improve findability.

In the next chapter I will introduce you to the online portal for DDC: WebDewey. Even if you do not currently have access to WebDewey, I encourage you to read on after you complete the Chapter 2 exercises.

CHAPTER 2 EXERCISES

Answer the following questions using the information provided in this chapter. You should not have to search any other source for the answer. Compare your answers to the answers provided in Appendix A.

1. I am cataloging a book about pancakes (641.8153) and biscuits (641.8157), which are discussed equally in the book. Under which DDC number should I class this book and why?

2. I am cataloging a book about the architecture of metal roofs. I could classify this book under 721.0447 (the use of metals as architectural material) or 721.5 (the architecture of roofs and roof structures). Under which DDC number should I class this book and why?
3. I am cataloging a book about the interior decoration of day care centers. I could classify this book under interior decoration (747) or day care centers (362.712). Under which DDC number should I class this book and why?
4. I am cataloging a book that discusses equally the topics of surfing (797.32), water skiing (797.35), and jet skiing (797.37), which are all under the broader topic of "other aquatic sports" (797.3). Under which DDC number should I class this book and why?
5. I am cataloging a book about the ethics of vice (179.8) and virtue (179.9), but the author focuses more on vice than virtue. Under which DDC number should I class this book and why?
6. I am cataloging a book on the effects of postpartum depression (618.76) on working mothers (331.44). Under which DDC number should I class this book and why?

NOTES

1. You can access the DDC Introduction by going here: OCLC, *Introduction to the Dewey Decimal Classification.* https://www.oclc.org/content/dam/oclc/dewey/versions/print/intro.pdf.
2. OCLC. *Introduction to the Dewey Decimal Classification.*
3. OCLC. *Introduction to the Dewey Decimal Classification* (p. 5).

3

WebDewey: The Online Portal to DDC

Now that you can identify basic principles of classification, let's move on to what's included in WebDewey.

As mentioned in Chapter 1, WebDewey is the main tool catalogers use to find and build DDC numbers. A subscription is required to access WebDewey, but OCLC offers a thirty-day free trial if you do not have access currently and want to give it a try (go to https://www.oclc.org/en/dewey/ordering.html to find out more). Once you have a username and password, log into WebDewey using those credentials. You can access WebDewey directly through this link: http://dewey.org/webdewey/. You should then see a screen that looks approximately like the one shown in Figure 3.1—don't worry if there are slight differences between your screen and mine.

Within WebDewey, you can type terms into the Search text box or click on the hyperlinked classes to access the DDC schedules. Note that the unabridged DDC 23rd edition is accessible on the left-hand side of the screen, and the abridged DDC 15th edition is on the right. The abridged DDC was designed with smaller library collections in mind (twenty thousand titles or less). It is not as robust as the unabridged DDC. In this book, I will use the unabridged 23rd edition of Dewey (also called DDC 23) when I provide examples and the answers to exercises, but I encourage you to consider what DDC numbers you would choose if you use the abridged edition.

At the top of the screen on the left-hand side there are buttons for "Search," "Advanced Search," and "Browse," actions that I will discuss in

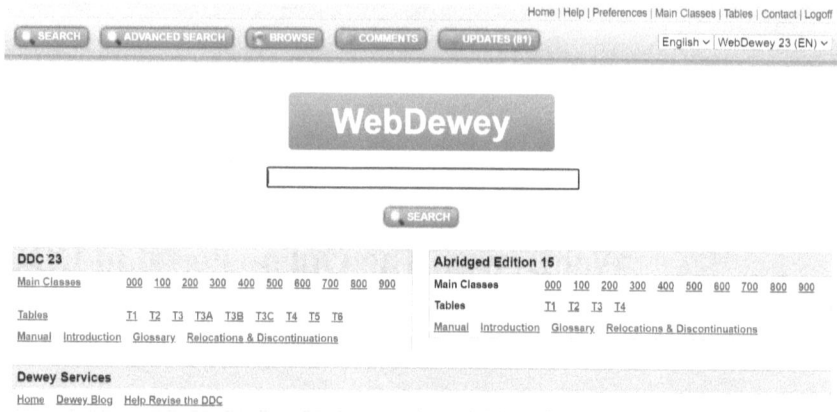

Figure 3.1. Home Page of WebDewey. *Source*: OCLC

greater detail in the next chapter. There are also buttons for "Comments" and "Updates." "Comments" are specific to the authorization number and provide a way for WebDewey users to save and edit comments on specific DDC numbers, such as notes about local decisions. Depending on your account, you will find options for a specific user to save comments that cannot be seen by others at the same institution, and other options to make comments visible and editable by anyone at an institution. "Updates" allows you to see a list of changes to DDC within the timeframe you specify. It defaults to the last thirty days, but you can input specific start and end dates to see updates from that timeframe. The "Updates" feature also provides an option to limit by notation and project; for example, if you want to see only the changes within the 300 class or a specific proposal for a change to a DDC number.

All the options I mention above remain at the top of the screen as you navigate WebDewey. In the upper right-hand corner of the screen are further options that also remain no matter where you navigate in WebDewey, including a link to "Home," which takes you back to the main home page (see Figure 3.2).

If you click on "Help," a pop-up help screen that contains links to many helpful resources will appear. The "Preferences" option allows you to change your WebDewey preferences (be careful with this if you share a WebDewey account with others). "Main Classes" and "Tables" take you to the DDC main classes and tables, respectively. "Contact" provides ad-

WebDewey: The Online Portal to DDC   23

| Home | Help | Preferences | Main Classes | Tables | Contact | Logoff |

| English ˅ | WebDewey 23 (EN) ˅ |

Figure 3.2. WebDewey Navigation Links. *Source:* OCLC

ditional OCLC support content and "Logoff" (as you can imagine) logs you out of WebDewey.

If we skip down to the bottom of the screen, there are several links under "Dewey Services." "Home" takes you to the Dewey Services homepage that contains information about DDC and WebDewey; "Dewey Blog" to the blog maintained by DDC editors and titled "025.431: The Dewey Blog," and "Help Revise the DDC" that takes you to a form you can complete if you would like to suggest changes or additions to DDC.

The options mentioned above are included in WebDewey as of this writing, but that may not always be the case. Therefore, if you don't see exactly what I see when you log into WebDewey, do not despair! WebDewey is a dynamic resource that changes over time to meet the needs of its users.

Back on the home page, let's look at some of the other links, particularly in the DDC23 box (see Figure 3.3).

If you click on the hyperlinked "Main Classes" within the DDC 23 area, you will see a list of the DDC main class numbers, which are also hyperlinked. Clicking on a caption, such as "Computer science, information & general works," will take you to a screen listing the divisions of that class (see Figure 3.4).

You can continue to click on the hyperlinks to go deeper into the hierarchy, which can be helpful if you are trying to find a DDC number for a specific topic but are unsure of the terminology you need to search for it. You can also go directly to a particular class (e.g., 000, 100, 200, etc.)

DDC 23

| Main Classes | 000 100 200 300 400 500 600 700 800 900 |
| Tables | T1 T2 T3 T3A T3B T3C T4 T5 T6 |
| Manual Introduction Glossary Relocations & Discontinuations |

Figure 3.3. DDC 23 Unabridged Links. *Source:* OCLC

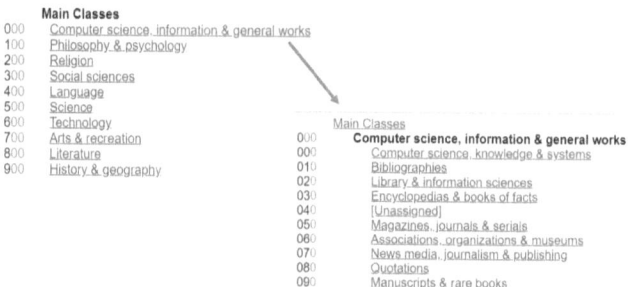

Figure 3.4. Classes to Divisions in 000. *Source*: OCLC

to explore that class in more depth. The same can be said of the tables (e.g., T1, T2, T3, etc.) that provide additional notation for DDC number building. Tables will be addressed in later chapters of this book (Chapters 7–11).

A direct link to the Manual can be found here as well. I will discuss the **Manual** in Chapter 5 of this book, so I won't go into detail about it here, but very briefly, it is a guide to the DDC that pays particular attention to challenges that arise when assigning DDC numbers and provides guidance when multiple DDC numbers seem applicable. The "Introduction" to DDC I mentioned previously is linked here, as well as the "Glossary" containing key terms used throughout the DDC and their definitions. As of this writing, when you click on "Relocations & Discontinuations," an Excel spreadsheet appears containing the relocations, discontinuations, and reused numbers from the 22nd edition of DDC to the 23rd edition.

Now that you have a better understanding of the content and features of WebDewey that you can access from the main page, let's go a little deeper into the website. The next chapter will cover how to search and browse in WebDewey, as well as explore the content and features you will encounter.

CHAPTER 3 EXERCISES

Answer the following questions using the information provided in this chapter and in WebDewey. Compare your answers to the answers provided in Appendix A.

1. Which WebDewey feature allows you to bring up a list of changes to DDC within the last thirty days?
2. Is there a way to add comments to class numbers in WebDewey?
3. How many tables are in the abridged DDC15?
4. True or False—There is a Dewey Blog maintained by Dewey editors.
5. If I don't currently have access to WebDewey, is there a way for me to try it out for free?
6. Go to the glossary and find the entry for "scope note." How does DDC define "scope note"?
7. From the WebDewey home page, click on the Technology class (600) and find the class number for Chemical Engineering. What is that class number?
8. What is the class number for Food technology within Chemical Engineering, within the Technology class?
9. From the WebDewey home page, browse the main DDC numbers, divisions, and possibly sections to find the topics the following class numbers represent:
    a. 210
    b. 328
    c. 750
    d. 913
    e. 093
    f. 549
    g. 498

4

Searching and Browsing in WebDewey

Imagine this: You are cataloging a book and need to assign a DDC number, or you want to double-check the DDC number in the existing bibliographic record you found for the book. Let's pretend that Figure 4.1 is the book in front of you, a nonfiction book about playing with toys.

Figure 4.1. *The Toys We Play With*. **Source**: Lauren Enjeti

28   Chapter 4

What now? Likely the most straightforward first step is to identify the main topic of the work—in this case, that appears to be "toys"—and search for that topic to see what we find in WebDewey. I mentioned in Chapter 2 that it is also helpful to determine the discipline in which the subject belongs, but one of the benefits of WebDewey is that we can search for the specific topic without having to know the discipline in advance. Knowing the discipline will still be helpful once we have search results to choose from.

If you are not on the main page of WebDewey, go back there and type "Toys" into the search box, and then click on Search. You may also type a DDC number into the search box if you are searching for a specific number.

When you perform a Search in WebDewey, you will see results that include that term anywhere within the schedules, so sometimes the results seem a little random, but they are actually ascending numerically by class number (see Figure 4.2).

You can see the DDC notation on the left and the caption for that number on the right that provides some, though certainly not necessarily all, contextual information. To find out more, click on the DDC number to go to that entry in the schedules.

The orange puzzle piece you see next to some entries indicates that the class number listed is a **built number**. Built numbers are created using a

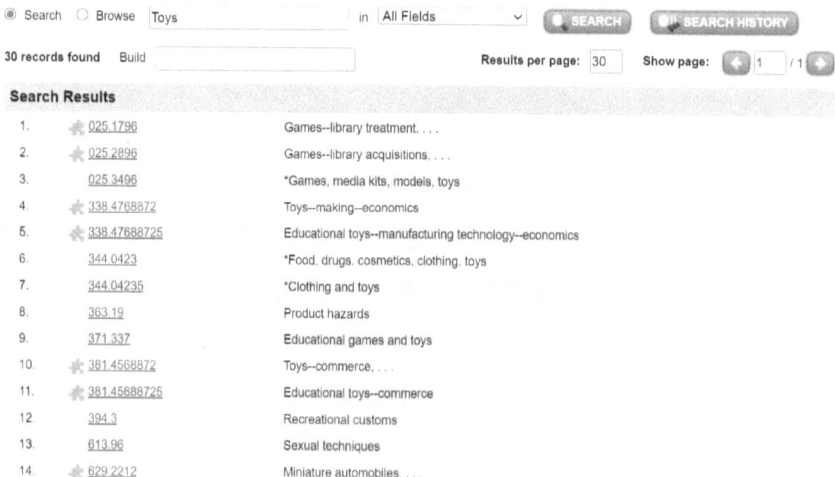

Figure 4.2.   Search Result for "Toys" in WebDewey. *Source*: OCLC

number from the DDC schedules and other notation, usually from one (or more) of the DDC tables. One of the benefits of using WebDewey is that it provides many (though not all) built numbers so that you do not have to build them yourself manually—a necessity when working with the DDC print volumes. I will cover DDC tables starting in Chapter 7, so don't worry about the built numbers and the tables right now, though certainly feel free to use them if they apply to what you are classifying.

Getting back to our "Toys" book and looking at the captions again, we see that some entries seem close to the topic of our book, but others . . . not so much. Since Search produces a result list with entries that contain "Toys" anywhere within that entry, you need to click on the hyperlinked class number to learn more about its meaning and context.

Note at the top of the screen the ability to choose "Search" or "Browse" next to the search box. "Toys" should still be there from our previous search, but now I want you to click on the "Browse" option, choose "Relative Index" from the dropdown menu, and click on the Search button to the right of the dropdown.

Browsing for a term in the **Relative Index** will retrieve entries for that term listed in alphabetical order. The Relative Index "arranges subject terms alphabetically and links the terms to the disciplines in which they appear in the schedules."[1] The Relative Index is a fantastic entry point into the DDC schedules, "entry point" being a key phrase here. Since DDC often provides guidance and instructions at each DDC number, you should always click through to the class number entry in the schedules for more information.

If you have a specific DDC number in mind, you can also browse that number, making sure you choose the "Dewey Numbers (With Captions)" option from the dropdown menu. However, let's return to the Relative Index browse for "Toys." Once you click on the Search button, you should see a result list like the one in Figure 4.3.

The Browse results provide a bit more context for us as we decide which class number to use for the book *The Toys We Play With*. The results are listed alphabetically by discipline within "Toys," starting with the more general "Toys" at 790.133, then "Toys" within advertising, cataloging, commerce, customs, and so on. I recommend that you try searching and browsing a topic in WebDewey to find a suitable class number, especially if you are still a Dewey novice.

Browse Results

Toyama-ken (Japan)	T2--52153
Toys	790.133
Toys--advertising	659.1968872
Toys--cataloging	025.3496
Toys--commerce	381.4568872
Toys--customs	394.3
Toys--library acquisitions	025.2896
Toys--library treatment	025.1796
Toys--making	688.72
Toys--making--collectibles	688.72075
Toys--making--economics	338.4768872
Toys--making--handicrafts	745.592
Toys--making--technology	688.72
Toys--product safety	363.19

Figure 4.3. Browse Results for *Toys*. *Source*: OCLC

We will start by clicking on the entry for just "Toys," which is 790.133, or you can go back to the home page of WebDewey and search for 790.133. Either way, you should see the screen in Figure 4.4, or a screen that looks very similar to it—sometimes the sections are arranged differently.

Let's look at where it says "Create built number" in the upper left-hand corner of my screenshot. This is a tool provided by WebDewey to add

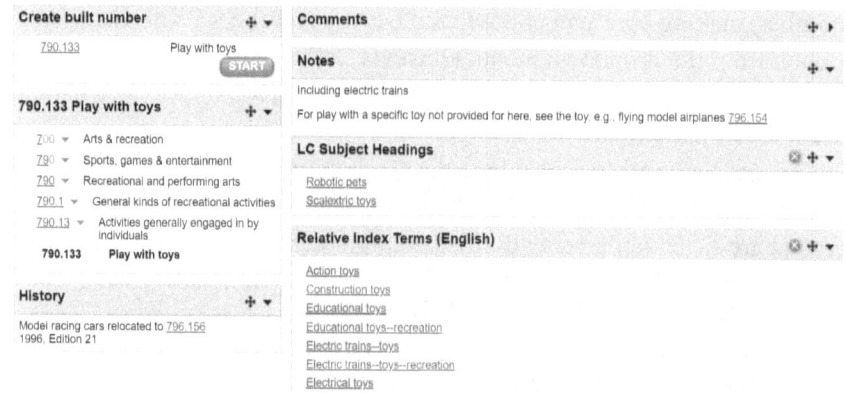

Figure 4.4. Entry for *Toys* in WebDewey. *Source*: OCLC

table notation to a DDC number if you want greater specificity. I will discuss the tables in Chapters 7–11. Feel free to play around with this tool but be careful to double-check the results.

Below the "Create built number" box in my screenshot is the class number within the DDC hierarchy, starting at the main class level (in this case, 700—Arts & Recreation) and going down through each level to the class number we chose, 790.133 (Play with toys). Note how each level is hyperlinked, which allows you to go back up the hierarchy to broader topics if you want to do so. Understanding where your class number is within the hierarchy can be helpful when determining which class number is best suited to the resource you are classifying. For example, if you are classifying a resource on toymaking, it is clear from the hierarchy that 790.133 is not the best choice for that resource, since 790.133 represents recreational play with toys, not making them.

Next to the hierarchy in my screenshot are the "Relative Index Terms" associated with this class number, which can be helpful for ascertaining the scope of a particular class number. For example, according to the Relative Index, resources about "Educational toys" should be classed here, if the focus is on the recreational aspect of these toys. Library of Congress Subject Headings (LCSH) correlated to 790.133 are included as well.

Even though it is not included in my screenshot on page 30, many DDC entries also have information about other subject headings that are related to the DDC number. Sometimes you will see Medical Subject Headings (MeSH) or Sears Subject Headings, for example, in addition to the LCSH. This information can be helpful if you need to find subject headings for a resource in addition to supplying a classification number, or if you want to double-check that a classification number fits an already chosen subject heading.

The "History" section, if populated, will provide a brief history of the class number in DDC. The class number 790.133 has the following history message: "Model racing cars relocated to 796.156, 1996, Edition 21." As DDC is a dynamic resource, it is not uncommon for topics to change location in the schedules.

Finally, let's examine the area titled "Notes" at 790.133. When using DDC, it is very important to pay close attention to the Notes area because frequently there are instructions that help you determine which class number to choose, which topics are included in the class number, and sometimes which topics are *not* included. For example, see the note that says, "For play with a specific toy not provided for here, see the toy, e.g., flying model airplanes 796.154" in the entry for 790.133. DDC is saying that there are other class numbers for toys of specific types that may not be within the scope of 790.133, like 796.154 for flying model planes, so you should search for the specific toy separately before choosing 790.133. The Notes area also says explicitly that resources about electric trains should be classified here, which is useful in case there is any doubt.

At the top of the 790.133 screen, you may have some additional orange buttons: MARC and Link to OPAC. If you click on the "MARC" button, you will see the class number from the page you are on within its MARC classification record (essentially an authority record for the class number). The "Link to OPAC" button is preprogrammed to take you to the Library of Congress's catalog listing of all works in their collection that are assigned the class number. According to the WebDewey help page, you can go to your "Preferences" to change or add to the Library of Congress catalog link. This feature is particularly handy if you want to confirm the types of resources to which a class number is typically assigned. If you search the catalog for a particular class number and there are only resources that seem nothing like the one you are cataloging, you should probably keep exploring WebDewey!

In the next chapter, I will discuss Notes in more depth, as well as introduce you to the Manual, which provides guidance on how to apply DDC numbers and how to decide between two (or sometimes more) numbers that may seem equally relevant to the resource you are classifying. But before you head to the next chapter, please test your knowledge of searching and browsing in WebDewey.

CHAPTER 4 EXERCISES

Answer the following questions using the information provided in this chapter and in WebDewey. Compare your answers to the answers provided in Appendix A.

1. What is a "built number" in Web Dewey?
2. True or False—The Relative Index retrieves entries in alphabetical order?

3. True or False—"Browse" and "Search" results are interchangeable and produce the same results.
4. True or False—"Notes" can be ignored when using Web Dewey.
5. How is the "Link to OPAC" at the top of the page handy and what can it be used for?

Searching WebDewey

Find the DDC number that best fits the following topics:

6. Neanderthals
7. Proverbs (not biblical) from around the world
8. World War I
9. Judaism
10. Loch Ness monster

Browsing DDC Numbers

Find the general topic associated with the following DDC numbers:

11. 133.12
12. 331.892
13. 814
14. 025.431
15. 413.17

Use WebDewey's Search and Browse to find an appropriate DDC number for nonfiction books with the following titles:

16. *Feng Shui for Small Spaces: An Introduction to Geomancy*
17. *Go Scuba Diving!*
18. *The History of the Ancient World: From the Earliest Accounts to the Fall of Rome*
19. *Crystallography for Beginners*
20. *Scholarships in Higher Education*
21. The Story of Juneteenth

NOTE

1. Chan, L. M., and Mitchell, J. S. (2003). *Dewey Decimal Classification: Principles and application*, 3rd edition. OCLC, p. 17.

5

Using Notes and the Manual

As mentioned in the previous chapter, the Notes area can be incredibly useful when identifying and/or making decisions about a DDC number, so it is critical to pay close attention to the Notes whenever they appear. Not all DDC numbers have notes associated with them, but many do. Here again is an example of Notes, but on the page for 523.8 (Stars)—see Figure 5.1.

According to the Notes area for 523.8, we should class comprehensive works on stars and galaxies at this class number. There are also several instructions on where to class related topics, such as the class number for the sun (523.7) and for galaxies more specifically and not as part of a larger discussion of stars and galaxies (523.112). The guidance extends to the "See also" notes that mention options for quasars (523.115) and extrasolar systems (523.24) if those are perhaps more appropriate for the work you are classifying.

The Notes area is the best reason I can give you to move beyond the search result list when you have found a promising class number. If included, the notes provide important guidance and the scope of the class

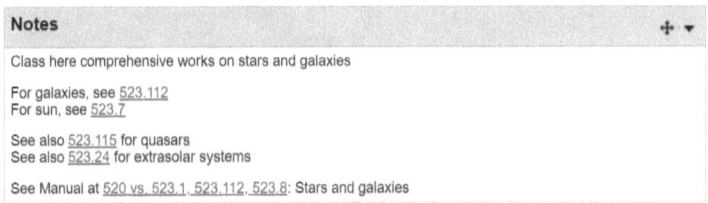

Figure 5.1. Notes Area of 523.8 (Stars). *Source*: OCLC

35

number, but they also sometimes include a link to the Manual, which offers even more in-depth information and advice. When in doubt about which class number to choose, use the Manual, if appropriate. In Chapter 3, I stated that the Manual is a guide to the DDC that pays particular attention to challenges that arise when assigning DDC numbers and provides guidance when multiple DDC numbers seem applicable. I want to come back to the Notes area, but let's delve into what the Manual has to offer first.

THE MANUAL

You can go directly to the Manual from the WebDewey home page by clicking on the hyperlinked "Manual" in the DDC 23 area (right under the Tables). You can also access the Manual from the Notes area of a class number, like you see in the notes for 523.8 (Stars) in Figure 5.1, or you can get to the Manual from certain search/browse results. Note in Figure 5.2 the orange book icon in the third search result—that icon indicates this result is an entry in the Manual.

If you click on that Manual entry, you should see a screen that has the information you see in Figure 5.3 (the order of the information may differ on your screen).

As mentioned previously, Manual entries are designed to help you make a classification decision in challenging areas, particularly when multiple class numbers seem applicable. The narrative within the note often provides additional context for a class number that should help you decide on the most appropriate number, but pay attention to the "If in doubt . . ." text, if present. This lovely phrase gives you an "out" in case

Search Results

1.	220.85238	Stars--Bible
2.	520	Astronomy and allied sciences
3.	520 vs. 523.1, 523.112, 523.8	Astronomy and allied sciences vs. The universe, galaxies, quasars vs. Galaxies vs. Stars
4.	523.1	The universe, galaxies, quasars
5.	523.112	Galaxies
6.	523.8	Stars
7.	523.80216	Star catalogs
8.	523[.80287]	Testing and measurement
9.	523.81-523.83	Properties and phenomena

Figure 5.2. Manual Entry in Search Results. *Source*: OCLC

Using Notes and the Manual 37

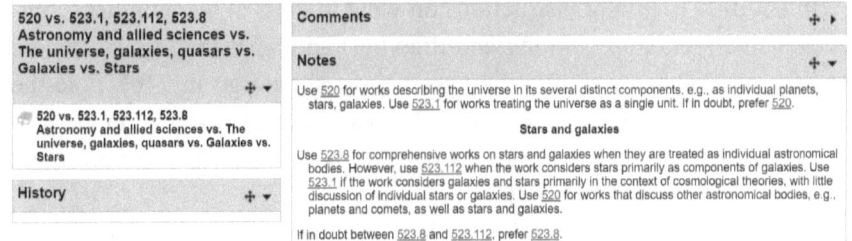

Figure 5.3. Manual Entry for 520 vs. 523.1, 523.112, 523.8. *Source*: **OCLC**

the note does not provide the information you need to make a decision. For example, in the Manual entry shown in Figure 5.3, it says to prefer 523.8 if you find there is not a clear winner between 523.8 and 523.112.

Not all class numbers have a Manual entry, but when in doubt, it is always a good idea to check the Manual just in case.

TABLES OF PREFERENCE WITHIN THE SCHEDULES

In addition to checking the Manual, it is very important to pay close attention to the (sometimes bountiful) information in the Notes area of a class number. Take, for example, the Notes area for DDC 750 (Painting and Paintings):

> Class here comprehensive works on painting and drawing.
> Unless other instructions are given, observe the following table of preference, e.g., an individual Canadian painter of landscapes 759.11 (not 758.10971), landscape painting in Canada 758.10971 (not 759.11):
> Individual painters and their work 759.1–759.9
> Techniques, procedures, apparatus, equipment, materials 751.2–751.6
> Iconography 753–758
> Specific forms 751.7
> Geographic treatment 759.1–759.9
> Periods of development 759.01–759.07
> Color 752
> Class comprehensive works on graphic arts, two-dimensional art in 740.
> Class painting in a specific decorative art with the art, for example, illumination of manuscripts and books 741.647.
> For drawing and drawings, see 741.

38   *Chapter 5*

In addition to giving instructions on what to class at this number (comprehensive works on painting and drawing) and what to class elsewhere (works on graphic arts, two-dimensional art should go in 740), note the inclusion of a "table of preference." Tables of preference pop up all over DDC, so let's explore one now so you can understand their purpose and what to do when you encounter one.

Let's say you need to assign a DDC number to a work on landscape painting in Canada (see Figure 5.4). Landscape painting is covered in the "Iconography" range of class numbers, the third option from the top of the table of preference on page 37. I know this from clicking on the hyperlinked 753–758 in the table, then 758 (Nature, architectural subjects and cityscapes, and other specific subjects), 758.1–758.5 (Nature), and 758.1

Figure 5.4. **Canadian Landscape Painting.** *Source*: Lauren Enjeti

(Landscapes). Additional notation is needed to include the "Canada" aspect (from Table 2, which we will discuss in Chapter 9), but the main point is that, even though this work has both iconographic ("landscapes") and geographic ("Canada") aspects that can be accommodated by Dewey, the table of preference at DDC 750 says to prefer the iconographic aspect in the primary class number (third in the table of preference) over the geographic aspect (fifth in the table of preference) because it is higher up in the table of preference.

If the work we are classifying is about an individual painter and their work, that is top priority according to the table of preference, and a DDC number between 759.1–759.9 should be chosen over any other. For example, as mentioned right above the table of preference at DDC 750, if the work we are classifying is about a Canadian landscape painter, we should choose the DDC number associated with individual Canadian painters (759.11) and not the DDC number associated with landscape painting in Canada (758.10971).

In the next chapter, I want to build on your "Notes" knowledge by focusing on notes that provide instructions on building DDC numbers using different parts of the schedules.

CHAPTER 5 EXERCISES

Answer the following questions using the information provided in this chapter and in WebDewey. Compare your answers to the answers provided in Appendix A.

1. At 736.4 (Wood carving), the Note area says that what topics are also included at this class number?
2. What kind of haunted places are included at 133.122? Also, what do I do if I am classifying a specific haunted place?
3. What DDC number should I assign to a work titled *Guide to Chamber Music*?
4. Go to 364 (Criminology) and review the table of preference in the Note area for that class number. Answer the following two questions using that table of preference:

a. According to the table of preference, should I class a work on the causes of specific types of criminal offenses in 364.1 or in 364.2?
b. According to the table of preference, where should I class a work on the history of discharged offenders?

5. Find the Manual entry for 551.5 versus 551.6 (Meteorology versus Climatology and weather) and answer the following questions:
   a. What class number should I choose if I am classifying a book titled *Climate and Weather* that also covers topics in meteorology?
   b. I need to classify a book about microclimatology. Should I choose 551.5 or 551.6?
   c. After reading through the 551.5 versus 551.6 entry in the Manual, I am still uncertain about which class number to choose. If I am in doubt, which class number should I choose?

6. Find the Manual entry for 004.678 versus 006.7, 025.042, 384.33 (Internet and World Wide Web) and answer the following questions:
   a. Which class number should I choose if the book I am classifying is about web page design?
   b. I have a book that is about the internet and World Wide Web that focuses more on information science than computer science. Should I class this work in 004.678 or 025.042?
   c. True or False—If I am in doubt about which class number to choose, I should prefer 006.7.

6

Number Building in DDC Using a Full or Part of a Number From the Schedules

As I discussed in previous chapters, DDC relies heavily on adding numbers to a base class number to provide specificity. Adding a "3" to 616 lets us clearly state that the work we are classifying is about diseases of the digestive system rather than about diseases generally. Often, the DDC schedules provide this specificity for us, but there will be instances when we have to do the work of adding numbers to achieve the specificity we desire. We have to "build" a DDC number, not unlike building a LEGO house, connecting individual blocks together.

As we will see in the next chapter, DDC number building using tables is a common way to add notation not already provided in the schedules. For example, we can place the Table 1 notation --03 (Dictionaries, encyclopedias, concordances) at the end of 567.9 (Dinosaurs) to create a DDC number for a dinosaur dictionary (567.903). However, there are other ways to build a DDC number; you will sometimes encounter specific instructions in the schedules that allow you to build without having to use Tables 1–6. Number building within the DDC schedule text itself can also provide specificity but can be straightforward or maddeningly challenging, depending on the topic. Let's walk through a few examples of this so you can learn the basics of how this works.

NUMBER BUILDING BY ADDING A FULL NUMBER

One example of number building is adding a full DDC number to another number. For instance, we can do this at DDC 026 (Libraries and archives devoted to specific subjects). If you go to 026 and click on 026.001–026.999 for "Specific subjects," you will see a Notes area that looks like the one in Figure 6.1.

To keep things simple for now, let's focus on the first line:

> Add to base number 026 notation 001–999, e.g., physics archives 026.53, medical libraries 026.61.

This instruction tells us that a DDC number for a specific subject library or archive needs to be built using the base number 026, and then add notation representing a specific subject at the end. WebDewey provides examples of a physics archive 026.53 (026 + "53" the first two digits of 530—Physics) and medical libraries 026.61 (026 + "61" the first two digits of 610—Medicine & Health). The instruction does not tell us explicitly to lop off the last zero of the subject area class number (53, not 530), but the examples make that clear. The actual rule is that we exclude any final zeroes if a decimal point is present, like in these examples:

> 026.5 = science libraries: 026 (libraries) + 500 (science)
> 026.78 = music libraries: 026 (libraries) + 780 (music)

Notes

Add to base number 026 notation 001-999, e.g., physics archives 026.53, medical libraries 026.61; then to the result add as follows:

01	Philosophy and theory
02	Miscellany
0285	Computer applications
	Do not use for digital libraries or digital archives; class in the number for library or archive without adding notation T1--0285 from Table 1, e.g., digital medical libraries 026.61
03-05	Standard subdivisions
06	Organizations
[068]	Management
	Do not use; class in 025.19
07-09	Standard subdivisions

Figure 6.1. Notes Area of 026.001-026.999 for (Specific subjects). *Source*: OCLC

However, not all notation that we assign to 026 will end with a zero like we see in the examples on page 42. A library with a focus on elementary education, for instance, should be assigned the class number 026.372 (372 representing elementary education).

NUMBER BUILDING BY ADDING PART OF A NUMBER

Number building in DDC does not always involve adding one full DDC number to another. Sometimes we add only a part of a DDC number to another number. Let's use "Animals" within folklore as an example of this process. If you go to 398.369 (Animals within Folklore), you will see the following instruction in the Notes area,

> Add to base number 398.369 the numbers following 59 in 592–599, e.g., rabbits 398.369932.

The base number 398.369 should be assigned to works that are about animal subjects in folklore, such as folklore featuring rabbits, cats, or elephants. The instruction says we need to add further notation to 398.369 to make it clear which animal is the focus. To do this, the instruction tells us that we should take notation from 592–599, which is a range of class numbers in Animals (Zoology) that provides class numbers for specific taxonomic groups of animals. The captions of these class numbers use, unfortunately for some of us, scientific nomenclature for the animal types, which I will discuss in more detail in a moment. But getting back to the "add" process, we don't take the entire class number from the 592–599 range—only the number(s) following the initial "59."

The example DDC provides is 398.369932, which is the class number of folklore featuring rabbits. Here is a breakdown:

398.369 (Animals within Folklore)
+
932 (the numbers following 59 in 599.32—Lagomorpha/Rabbits)
=
398.369932 (Rabbits in Folklore)

To double-check this example, I browsed for rabbits in the 592–599 range. I don't know about you, but I did not know the scientific term for rabbits (Lagomorpha) and struggled to find rabbits, even knowing it should be somewhere in the 592–599 range of class numbers. Instead of continuing to browse 592–599, I searched for "rabbits" using the general search tool and found 599.32, labeled "Lagomorpha" in the search results, but I knew it had to be the correct class number because it is the only number in the list that fits in the 592–599 range. Browsing for "rabbits" in the Relative Index provided 599.32 as well, but with the caption of "Rabbits," which was much more helpful.

It was nice having the example provided as guidance, but we cannot rely on DDC always providing the examples we need. Let's try this process again with an animal not included in a DDC example—elephants.

Once again, we start with the base number 398.369 for animals within folklore and the instructions at 398.369 that say, "Add to base number 398.369 the numbers following 59 in 592–599." Therefore, we need to find the class number for elephants within that 592–599 range. Like I mentioned previously, those unfamiliar with scientific nomenclature may find it easier to search for the animal directly as opposed to browsing through 592–599. When I search for "elephants," the only non-built result I get (no orange puzzle piece) is 599.67—Proboscidea (see Figure 6.3).

Figure 6.2. *Elephants in Folklore. Source*: Lauren Enjeti

If you click on 599.67 (Proboscidea), the Notes area tells us to "Class here elephants." Success! Once again, try browsing the topic in the Relative Index as well if you are uncertain.

Next, we follow the instruction at 398.369 to "Add to base number 398.369 the numbers following 59 in 592–599." The numbers following the initial 59 in 599.67 are 967. Therefore,

Number Building in DDC Using a Full or Part of a Number From the Schedules 45

● Search	○ Browse	elephants		in All Fields ∨	
7 records found	Build				

Search Results

1.	333.95967	Elephants--resource economics
2.	569.67	Proboscidea--paleozoology, . . .
3.	599.67	*Proboscidea
4.	599.671392	Young animals--elephants, . . .
5.	636.967	Elephants--animal husbandry
6.	639.97967	Elephants--conservation technology
7.	799.2767	Elephants--big game hunting

Figure 6.3. Search Results for "Elephants" in WebDewey. *Source:* OCLC

398.369 (Animals in Folklore)

+

967 (Elephants)

=

398.369967 (Elephants in Folklore)

MORE COMPLEX NUMBER BUILDING INSTRUCTIONS

Before we move on, I want to discuss number building with the schedule text similar to what we have been doing, but with an additional layer of complexity. Take a look at the Notes area for the DDC class number range of 633–635 (Specific plant crops with Agriculture) in Figure 6.4.

Notes

Add to each subdivision identified by * as follows:
    1-6   Cultivation and harvesting
        Add the numbers following 631.5 in 631.51-631.56, e.g., harvesting 5
        For special cultivation methods, see notation 8 from this table
    7   Varieties and kinds
        Class specific techniques of cultivation and harvesting specific varieties in notation 1-6 from this table
        Class fertilizers, soil conditioners, growth regulators for specific varieties in notation 89 from this table
        Class injuries, pests, diseases of specific varieties in notation 9 from this table
    8   Special cultivation methods; fertilizers, soil conditioners, growth regulators
    81-87   Special cultivation methods
        Add to 8 the numbers following 631.58 in 631.581-631.587, e.g., organic farming 84
    89   Fertilizers, soil conditioners, growth regulators
        Add to 89 the numbers following 631.8 in 631.81-631.89, e.g., compost 8975
    9   Injuries, diseases, pests
        Add to 9 the numbers following 632 in 632.1-632.9, e.g., insect pests 97

Class comprehensive works in 630

See Manual at 633-635

Figure 6.4. Notes Area for 633–635. *Source:* OCLC

Here we have a table of instructions and not a single sentence—yikes! In this example, DDC is providing options for us to build class numbers for specific plant crops that consider aspects like cultivating and harvesting plant crops, special cultivation methods of plant crops, and diseases that can affect plant crops, but only for class numbers in the 633–635 number range that have an asterisk (*) next to them. Let's walk through an example that applies these instructions.

Let's say I am cataloging a fascinating book about oats. Searching for "oats" that appears in the 633–635 class number range produces 633.13 (see reproduction below).

633–635 Specific plant crops
    633 Field and plantation crops
        633.1 Cereals
            633.13 *Oats

Is there an asterisk (*) next to Oats on the left-hand side of the page? Yes, there is! And notice the Notes area says to "*Add as instructed under 633–635," which is a reference to the table we just saw at 633–635. However, if the book we are cataloging is only about oats generally, we can stop here—no need to add further notation to 633.13 if the book does not go into depth about cultivation methods, diseases, etc. But what if our book is, indeed, about a more specific "oat" topic, such as the harvesting of oats? What do we do next?

If we keep 633.13 (Oats) in our head and journey back to the instructions at 633–635 (see Figure 6.4), we see the following instruction: "Cultivation and harvesting. Add the numbers following 631.5 in 631.51–631.56, e.g., harvesting 5."

Believe it or not, this scenario is similar to our elephants in folklore example on pages 44 and 45. We want to add to our base class number for oats (633.13) additional notation for harvesting, but we need to go to 631.51–631.56 to find harvesting, which is 631.55 (see below for a reproduction of the class numbers at 631.5—Cultivation and harvesting).

631.5 Cultivation and harvesting
631.51 Soil working (Tillage)
631.52 Production of seeds, bulbs, tubers, new varieties

631.53 Plant propagation
631.54 Grafting, pruning, training
631.55 Harvesting
631.56 Operations subsequent to harvesting
631.57 Varieties and kinds of organisms used in agriculture
631.58 Special methods of cultivation

Since the instructions at 633–635 say to add only the numbers following 631.5, we grab the "5" at the end of 631.55. Our base class number is 633.13 (Oats)—we take the "5" from the end of harvesting (631.55) and place it at the end of our base number: **633.135**. We now have a class number to assign to our book on oat harvesting!

I highly recommend taking time to practice number building within the DDC schedule text before moving on to the next chapter.

CHAPTER 6 EXERCISES

Answer the following questions using the information provided in this chapter and in WebDewey. Compare your answers to the answers provided in Appendix A.

Exercises with Number Building by Adding a Full Number

1. Use the instruction at 418.03 (Translating materials on specific subjects) to create class numbers for the following topics:
   a. Translating materials on Aristotelian philosophy
   b. Translating materials on astronomy (generally, within Science)
   c. Translating materials on the passage of legislation
2. Use the instruction at 659.19001–659.19999 (subdivisions for specific kinds of organizations, products, services within Advertising) to create class numbers for the following topics:
   a. Advertising jewelry
   b. Advertising statistical software
   c. Advertising pet food

Exercises with Number Building by Adding Part of a Number

3. Use the instructions at 205.6 (Specific moral issues, sins, vices, virtues) to create class numbers for the following topics:
   a. Morality of the consumption of alcoholic beverages
   b. Morality of the gambling business
   c. Morality of nuclear weapons and nuclear war
4. Use the instructions at 641.63–641.67 (Cooking food derived from plant crops and domesticated animals) to create class numbers for the following topics:
   a. Cooking with grapes
   b. Cooking with kola nuts
   c. Cooking with turkey

Exercises with More Complex Number Building

5. Use the instruction at 387.21–387.29 (Specific types of ships) to create class numbers for the following topics:
   a. Hand-propelled and towed craft
   b. Ferryboats
   c. Warships

7

Advanced Class Number Building Using Table 1—Part 1—The Basics of Adding Standard Subdivisions

As we saw in the last chapter, number building in DDC is important when you want to assign classification numbers that capture a resource's subject matter more specifically. The most common way to build DDC numbers is through the tables. There are six tables in the unabridged DDC—Tables 1–6—with Table 3 having three additional sub-tables 3A, 3B, and 3C.

Table notation is easy to spot in DDC as it always begins with a single (-) or double-dash (--) preceding the numbers and often begins with a zero, a facet indicator that signifies a change from primary to secondary topics. Examples include --05 and --0727. Table notation should never be used alone—it must always be placed at the end of a DDC number.[1] An example of a built DDC number using Table 1 notation is 567.903, representing a dinosaur dictionary (see Figure 7.1).

567.9 (DDC number for dinosaurs)
+
--03 (Dictionary from Table 1)
=

567.903 (Dinosaur dictionary—remove the double dash from the beginning of the Table 1 notation before placing it after the DDC number)

In this chapter, I want to focus on Table 1, which contains what DDC calls the **standard subdivisions**. The standard subdivisions are notations that "represent frequently recurring physical forms (dictionaries, periodicals) or approaches (history, research) applicable to any subject or discipline"[2]

Figure 7.1. *Dinosaur Dictionary. Source*: Lauren Enjeti

and are not the main topic of a work—they supplement it. The main topic of the dinosaur dictionary, for example, is dinosaurs. Dictionary is the physical form. The Table 1 standard subdivisions are the most common notations used to build DDC numbers, so if you have time to familiarize yourself with only one DDC table, this is the one to choose!

Assigning notation from other DDC tables works similarly, but with many caveats. Just like the DDC schedules, there are extensive instructions that should be consulted prior to assigning table notation. However, before we get too far into the weeds of these instructions, let's discuss how to find the DDC tables and look at what is included in Table 1.

Go back to the home page of WebDewey (clicking on the "Search" button at the top of the screen will get you there) and look at the line that starts with "Tables." The rest of the line contains T1, T2, and so forth, each hyperlinked so you can go directly to a specific table. If you click on the hyperlinked "Tables" you will see a list of all the tables used in DDC, reproduced here:

Table 1. Standard Subdivisions
Table 2. Geographic Areas, Historical Periods, Biography
Table 3. Subdivisions for the Arts, for Individual Literatures, for Specific Literary Forms
Table 3A. Subdivisions for Works by or about Individual Authors
Table 3B. Subdivisions for Works by or about More than One Author
Table 3C. Additional Notation for Arts and Literature
Table 4. Subdivisions of Individual Languages and Language Families
Table 5. Ethnic and National Groups
Table 6. Languages

Click on Table 1 and you will see this list of entries within the table (see Figure 7.2).

Notice how each line begins with T1--0x, making it clear that we are using Table 1 and the double dash (--), indicating that whatever numbers follow are from a table and are not class numbers. I recommend browsing the Table 1 standard subdivisions to learn more about what is covered.

Click on each of the subdivisions, and if there are no additional subdivisions that further narrow the topic, you will see a screen similar to what we see in entries within the DDC schedules, with a Notes area, the subdivision's place within the Table 1 hierarchy, and Relative Index terms associated with the subdivision.

Some of the Table 1 standard subdivisions can be quite complex, and you will need to dig deep into the hierarchy to determine which notation is applicable. For example, if you click on T1--02 Miscellany, you will see this list:

T1--0 Table 1. Standard Subdivisions	
T1--0	Table 1. Standard Subdivisions
T1--01	Philosophy and theory
T1--02	Miscellany
T1--03	Dictionaries, encyclopedias, concordances
T1--04	Special topics
T1--05	Serial publications
T1--06	Organizations and management
T1--07	Education, research, related topics
T1--08	Groups of people
T1--09	History, geographic treatment, biography

Figure 7.2. DDC Table 1. *Source:* OCLC

T1--02 Miscellany
T1--0202 Synopses and outlines
T1--0207 Humorous treatment
T1--0208 Audiovisual treatment
T1--021 Tabulated and related materials
T1--022 Illustrations, models, miniatures
T1--023 The subject as a profession, occupation, hobby
T1--024 The subject for people in specific occupations
T1--025 Directories of persons and organizations
T1--(026) Law
T1--027 Patents and identification marks
T1--028 Auxiliary techniques and procedures; apparatus, equipment, materials
T1--029 Commercial miscellany

You can keep clicking on the hyperlinked entries to learn more about what is included here. Click on T1--022 (Illustrations, models, miniatures) and you will see more options:

T1--022 Illustrations, models, miniatures
T1--0222 Pictures and related illustrations
T1--0223 Maps, plans, diagrams
T1--0228 Models and miniatures

Click on T1--0222 (Pictures and related illustrations), which is as far as we can go down this branch of the hierarchy and notice the note in the upper right-hand corner. As we saw in the schedules, there is further information here that helps us determine if it is appropriate to use this Table 1 notation. We can use --0222 for "cartoons, drawings, pictorial charts and designs, sketches." This information will appear in regular searches in WebDewey as well. If I perform a Search for "cartoons" for example, I see the results in Figure 7.3 (note the second entry).

Now that you know how to search and browse Table 1, let's apply the Table 1 notation to DDC numbers. Let's say we are classifying a pictorial book about birds. Birds (Aves) are represented by DDC number 598. Unless there are instructions at the class number that state that you cannot add standard subdivisions, you can add them to most any class number in DDC. As we found during our explorations above, --0222 is the Table 1 notation for "Pictures and related illustrations."

Advanced Class Number Building Using Table 1—Part 1

1.	T1--0207	Humorous treatment
2.	T1--0222	Pictures and related illustrations
3.	T1--08	Groups of people
4.	T1--08:022	Illustrations
5.	T1--0901-T1--0905	Historical periods
6.	T1--0901-T1--0905:022	Illustrations
7.	T1--0901-T1--0905:09022	Illustrations
8.	T1--093-T1--099	Specific continents, countries, localities; extraterrestrial worlds
9.	T1--093-T1--099:022	Illustrations
10.	T1--093-T1--099:09009022	Illustrations

Figure 7.3. Search Results for Cartoons. *Source*: OCLC

All you need to do to include the Table 1 notation is to place it at the end of the chosen class number, like this, leaving off the double dash (--):

598 + --0222 = 598.0222

("+" in this context means to place the notation at the end of the class number. It does **not** mean that you should literally add 598 and 0222 together)

The number 598.0222 represents a resource that is a heavily illustrated work about birds.

Generally, you are safe to add Table 1 notation to most classification numbers you find in the schedules, but there are, of course, exceptions to everything I just told you.

THE EXCEPTIONS

There are many "exceptions" to the general rule of adding Table 1 notation as discussed above, so it is somewhat odd to call them exceptions. Most of these exceptions relate to the modification of the number of zeroes in the Table 1 notation, but sometimes adding Table 1 notation is problematic for more conceptual or practical reasons. For instance, sometimes a standard subdivision is already embedded in the class number, such as with class number 443, which represents French dictionaries. Adding Table 1 notation for dictionaries (--03) to 443 would be redundant and therefore should not be done. In addition, your library may not need the specificity provided by table notation, especially if you have few items in a subject area or have a strict policy of keeping DDC numbers short. Clearly you need to use your judgment and/or institutional policy when deciding when it is or is not appropriate to add certain notation.

Dropping Terminal Zeros

Unless other instructions are given, the terminal zeros in a main class or division number should be dropped before adding a standard subdivision. If a main class number is used, drop two zeros; drop one zero in division class numbers.

For example:

An encyclopedia of philosophy
100 (Philosophy) + --03 (encyclopedias from Table 1) = **103**, not 100.03
A journal of mathematics
510 (Mathematics) + --05 (serial publications from Table 1) = **510.5**, not 510.05

However, be on the lookout for class numbers that do not follow this pattern. For example, look at the entry for physics at 530, which clearly signifies that the division zero should be retained (for example, 530.02, not 530.2).

Additionally, the following five main classes do not follow the "dropping zeros" exception and therefore you can add the standard subdivision notation normally:

- **000 (Computer Science, Information, General Works)**—class numbers 003–006 are reserved for systems and computer science (e.g., book collecting = 002.075, not 002.75)
- **200 (Religion)**—class numbers 201–209 are reserved for specific aspects of religion (e.g., religious education = 200.7, not 207)
- **300 (Social Sciences)**—class numbers 301–307 are reserved for specific sociology topics (e.g., philosophy of social science = 300.1, not 301)

- **700 (Arts & Recreation)**—class numbers 701–709 are limited to standard subdivisions of fine and decorative arts (e.g., encyclopedia of the arts = 700.3, not 703)
- **900 (History & Geography)**—class numbers 901–909 are reserved for standard subdivisions of history alone (e.g., a serial publication on history & geography = 900.5, not 905)

Adding Zeros

Sometimes the schedules will note that an *additional zero* should be included in order to avoid an existing conflict with special topics class numbers. Pay close attention to the hierarchy at the DDC number as it is usually clear when an additional zero is needed. For example, look at DDC 636.3 (Sheep and goats):

636.3 Sheep and goats
636.3001–636.3009 Standard subdivisions
636.301–636.308 Specific topics in husbandry of sheep and goats together, of sheep alone
636.31 Sheep for specific purposes
636.32–636.38 Specific breeds of sheep
636.39 Goats

This entry is saying that 636.3001 through 636.3009 (with the additional zero) are used for the Table 1 standard subdivisions because 636.301 through 636.308 (with only one zero) are currently reserved for specific topics in the husbandry of sheep and goats together, or of sheep alone (such as sheep care and sheep ranches). In order to avoid confusion, DDC says to add an additional zero to the standard subdivisions. In other words, a heavily illustrated book about sheep would have the class number 636.300222 and not 636.30222. Libraries with large collections of works

Figure 7.4. Sheep. *Source*: **Lauren Enjeti**

on animal husbandry or agriculture, for example, will need to pay close attention to these instructions.

Limited Table 1 Usage

The final exception to adding Table 1 notation normally to a DDC number is instruction to either exclude standard subdivisions altogether or add them under limited circumstances. For example, the note at 025.42 (Classification and shelflisting) says that "Standard subdivisions are added for classification and shelflisting together, for classification alone." Therefore, you can add a standard subdivision to 025.42 if the work you are cataloging is about both classification and shelflisting, or *only* about classification, but not for a work *only* about shelflisting. This type of instruction is quite common for classification numbers that represent multiple topics, so pay close attention to the notes if you need to assign one. The reason for these types of notes is largely due to what is called "approximating the whole," a concept that I will discuss in more depth at the beginning of the next chapter.

The Table 1 standard subdivisions are great at providing additional specificity but are often not needed to capture the main topic of the resource being classified. Therefore, if you are looking to save time and/or spine label space, consider leaving off standard subdivisions. There is more I want to tell you about Table 1, so Chapter 8 will continue the discussion! Complete the exercises before you move on.

CHAPTER 7 EXERCISES

Answer the following questions using the information provided in this chapter and in WebDewey. Compare your answers to the answers provided in Appendix A.

1. True or False—Table notations can be used alone.
2. True or False—It is okay to leave off the standard subdivision to save time and/or spine label space.

Find the Table 1 notation that represents the following topics:

3. Philosophy and theory
4. Management of materials
5. Patents and identification marks
6. Statistical methods

For each of the following topics, find the appropriate class number and Table 1 notation:

7. An encyclopedia of zodiac signs.
8. A work on the classification of commercially produced beer and ale.
9. Historical research on public libraries.
10. A work on psychology as a profession.
11. A humorous treatment of horses (from the animal husbandry perspective).

Deconstruct the meaning of each DDC number below. Each contains a class number and a Table 1 notation.

12. 300.71
13. 211.012
14. 795.403

NOTES

1. There are exceptions to this rule, such as the placement of table notation after "special notation" and not the DDC number itself. I will provide further explanation of this exception in Chapter 8.
2. Chan and Mitchell, *Dewey Decimal Classification*, p. 81.

8

Advanced Class Number Building Using Table 1—Part 2—Approximating the Whole, Groups of People, Biography, and Historical Periods

The last chapter provided you with the basics of DDC number building using Table 1 standard subdivisions. You may have noticed that I did not mention --08 (Groups of people) and --09 (History, geographic treatment, biography). I want to cover those in this chapter, as well as the Table 1 table of preference, approximating the whole, and Table 1 special notation.

APPROXIMATING THE WHOLE

Let's start with **approximating the whole**, the idea that the class number you choose should align as closely as possible to the subject of the work you are cataloging. According to the DDC instructions, you may add a standard subdivision to any class number that approximates the whole of the subject or discipline, unless instructed otherwise. We saw this in the last chapter in the 025.42 (Classification and shelflisting) example. As a reminder, the note at 025.42 says, "Standard subdivisions are added for classification and shelflisting together, for classification alone." This note is telling us that a work on both classification and shelflisting, as well as a work on only classification, approximate the whole of the meaning of the class number; a work solely on shelflisting does not approximate the whole. Therefore, 025.4205 (--05 meaning serial publications) is appropriate to assign to a work on both classification and shelflisting, as well as a work solely on classification. We could assign 025.42 to a work solely on shelflisting, but we may not add any standard subdivisions to the class number.

Categories of topics that approximate the whole include:

1. Topics in dual headings
2. Topics in multiterm headings that are so designated with a standard subdivisions-are-added note
3. Topics in class-here notes
4. Topics that represent more than half the content of a heading
5. Topics that cover at least three subdivisions of the number
6. Topics coextensive with topics that approximate the whole[1]

Figure 8.1. *18th Century Elf Folktales. Source*: Lauren Enjeti

Occasionally DDC provides in notes clear guidance on whether a class number approximates the whole. For example, 398.2 (Folk literature) has a note that states, "Standard subdivisions may be added to subdivisions of this number for any topic even if the subject of the work does not approximate the whole, e.g., 18th century folktales about elves 398.2109033."

The class number 398.2109033 (Eighteenth century folktales about elves) is a good example of a class number built using --09 in Table 1 to include time period, which I will return to after I explain the Table 1 table of preference and groups of people (--08).

Table 1 Table of Preference

The introduction to DDC clearly states that you should not "add multiple standard subdivisions to the same number except when specifically instructed to do so" or in special cases, such as the use of "special notation" with standard subdivisions that I will discuss momentarily. Therefore, if we have, say, a resource that is both a serial publication (--05) and contains research (--07), we cannot include standard subdivisions representing both aspects to the base class number. Instead, DDC wants you to choose between the two Table 1 notations. The Table 1 table of preference helps you make this choice.

The Table 1 table of preference can be found by clicking on Table 1 from the WebDewey main menu and scrolling down about halfway through the notes (see Figure 8.2).

The purpose of the table of preference is to help the classifier choose a standard subdivision when multiple could be added to the class number, except for instances when the rule of application and rule of zero apply (see Chapter 2 of this text to review these two rules). Select the standard subdivision that is higher up in the table of preference.

Let's say we are classifying the dinosaur dictionary (567.903) from Chapter 7 of this book but add that it is a heavily illustrated dictionary. We have to choose between notation that indicates that the book is a dictionary and that it is illustrated. Looking at the table of preference above, is "dictionaries" (--03) or "illustrations" (--022) closer to the top of the table of preference?

Unless other instructions are given, observe the following table of preference, e.g., communication in education and research T1--07 (not T1--014):

Special topics	T1--04
Biography	T1--092
Auxiliary techniques and procedures; apparatus, equipment, materials	T1--028
Education, research, related topics (except T1--074, T1--075)	T1--07
Management	T1--068
Philosophy and theory	T1--01
The subject as a profession, occupation, hobby	T1--023
The subject for people in specific occupations	T1--024
Directories of persons and organizations	T1--025
Patents and identification marks	T1--027
Commercial miscellany	T1--029
Organizations	T1--0601-T1--0609
Organizations (without subdivision)	T1--06
Groups of people	T1--08
Specific continents, countries, localities; extraterrestrial worlds	T1--093-T1--099
Areas, regions, places in general	T1--091
Historical periods	T1--0901-T1--0905
Archaeology	T1--09009
Museums, collections, exhibits	T1--074
Museum activities and services	T1--075
Illustrations, models, miniatures	T1--022
Tabulated and related materials	T1--021
Synopses and outlines	T1--0202
Humorous treatment	T1--0207
Audiovisual treatment	T1--0208
Dictionaries, encyclopedias, concordances	T1--03
Serial publications of history, geographic treatment, biography	T1--09005
History and geographic treatment (without subdivision)	T1--09
Serial publications	T1--05

The rule of application overrides the table of preference above. For example, teaching financial management in hospital administration is classed in 362.110681, not 362.11071. The rule of zero also overrides this table of preference when standard subdivisions are displaced to notation outside the regular sequence of standard subdivisions. For example, management of prisons in Great Britain is classed in 365.941068, not 365.068

Figure 8.2. Table 1 Table of Preference. *Source:* OCLC

If you said "illustrations," you win a gold star! "Illustrations, models, miniatures" is higher on the table of preference than "Dictionaries, encyclopedias, concordances." Therefore, we need to modify the illustrated dinosaur dictionary class number to 567.9022—dinosaurs (567.9) plus notation for illustrations (--022) and leave off the notation for dictionaries (--03). Further practice using the table of preference is located in the Chapter 8 exercises that begin on page 70.

Groups of People (--08)

The Groups of people (--08) in Table 1 provides classifiers a way to include notation specifically relating to characteristics of people, such as age, gender, occupations, and ethnicity, in addition to the topic represented in the base class number (see representation of Table 1 --08).

> **T1--08** Groups of people
> **T1--08:01** Forecasting and forecasts
> **T1--08:02** Statistics and illustrations
> **T1--08:03** Dictionaries, encyclopedias, concordances
> **T1--08:05** Serial publications
> **T1--08:07** Museums, collections, exhibits; collecting objects
> **T1--08:09** History and geographic treatment
> **T1--0801–T1--0809** Forecasting, statistics, illustrations, dictionaries, encyclopedias, concordances, serials, museums and collecting, history and geographic treatment
> **T1--081–T1--088** Groups of people by specific attributes
> **T1--089** Ethnic and national groups

For now, ignore the first seven entries and look at T1--081–T1--088 (Groups of people by specific attributes) and T1--089 (Ethnic and national groups). I encourage you to click on the hyperlinks to expand and explore the options presented. The first step is to determine the appropriate class number for the work in hand, then add the notation for the group involved. For example, if I am classifying a book called *Chess for Children*, I would find the class number for "chess" first (794.1) and then find the Table 1 notation that corresponds to "children." Next, click on T1--081–T1--088

(Groups of people by specific attributes). Then, click on T1--083–T1--084 to expand the section on "Age groups" and choose "Young people." When you do this, you see further options for specific age ranges of young people, starting with "Infants" and ending with "Young people twelve to twenty."

If the book we are classifying is for all children, not just children of particular ages, then what do we do? Thankfully the notes section holds the answer. T1--083 (Young people) has a "Class here children" note, so we can confidently place --083 at the end of the class number for "chess":

794.1 (Chess)
+
--083 (Young people—including children generally)
=
794.1083 (Chess for children)

Biographical Treatment (--092)

Biographies are different from the groups of people notation we discussed in the last section because they focus on individuals (such as Martin Luther King Jr.) rather than general group characteristics (such as men and Christians). Some libraries choose not to use this feature of Dewey because the DDC notation places the biography in the discipline of the biography's subject rather than in one "biography" class area. It is not uncommon for libraries to physically locate all biographies in one designated area rather than have them scattered in different locations.

In the notes for Biography (T1--092), it says that biography includes, "Autobiography, description and critical appraisal of work, diaries, reminiscences, correspondence of people regardless of area, region, or place who are part of the subject or who study the subject, e.g., biographers, collectors, leaders and followers, practitioners and clients, scholars."

To build a biography class number, first find the class number associated with the person's "most noted contribution," according to the Manual entry for --092. If a person's most noted contribution is being a swimmer, then find the DDC number for "swimming" (797.21) and then place --092 at the end of the class number:

797.21 (Swimming)
+
--092 (Biography)
=
797.21092 (Biography of a swimmer)

Class numbers that end with a zero should drop a zero when adding --092 unless instructions say otherwise. For example, a biography of a doctor (Medicine = 610) should be assigned 610.92, not 610.092.

There are exceptions to the use of --092, of course. The notes at --092 also say:

> Observe instructions not to use T1--092 that apply to 180–190, 759, 809, 810–890. (The instructions for 810–890 are found under notation T3B--09 from Table 3B)
>
> Do not use T1--092 for a person whose name is used in a schedule heading, e.g., class Muḥammad the Prophet in 297.63 (not 297.63092).

Therefore, you need to be careful when classifying biographies to double-check the DDC number associated with the subject of the biography and note any exceptions that apply.

In addition to adhering to the exceptions, probably one of the more challenging aspects of classifying biographies is determining the class number to start with for the subject of the biography. Someone whose most noted contribution is swimming is likely safe to class in 797.21092, but what about those who had many notable contributions throughout their life, like Benjamin Franklin, a printer, inventor, writer, statesman, and much more? Once again, the Manual at --092 provides helpful advice:

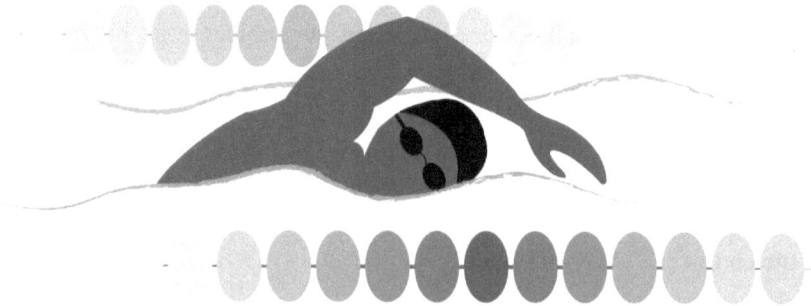

Figure 8.3.   Swimmer. *Source*: Lauren Enjeti

If the person made approximately equal contributions to a number of fields, use the number for the subject that provides the best common denominator, giving some extra consideration to the person's occupation.

Regarding public figures, the Manual recommends using class numbers 930–990 for persons who have held a variety of offices and consider their impact on history or specific causes. Biographies of Benjamin Franklin, for example, are most often classed in 973.3092, with 973.3 representing the Periods of Revolution and Confederation, 1775–1789 in the United States, emphasizing his contribution to the formation of the new country.

When assigning a class number to a biography, I recommend checking your catalog or another library's catalog, to see how other biographies of that person have been classed, assuming other biographies exist. I also highly recommend reviewing the Manual at T1--092 for further instructions on how to classify in this area.

For a collective biography (a biography of two or more people), use --0922. For instance, a collective biography of multiple swimmers would be assigned the class number 797.210922—exactly the same as the individual biography number but with an additional "2" at the end.

QUICK TIP . . .

Local practices abound for biographies, so pay close attention to where your library places these works. Some libraries will use 920 generally for biographies, or simply assign BIO or B in biography call numbers, keeping all biographies together, regardless of the biography subject.

Table 1—Historical Periods (--0901–0908)

The historical periods section of Table 1 (--0901–0908) is needed when you are classifying a work in which time period is emphasized, such as a book about fashion in the 1960s, or the eighteenth century elf folktale book mentioned earlier in this chapter. This section within Table 1 is depicted in Figure 8.4.

I want to set aside discussion of the first six entries and focus on the last five: T1--0901 (To 499 CE) to T1--0905 (twenty-first century, 2000–

T1--0901-T1--0905 Historical periods	
T1--0 ▾	Table 1. Standard Subdivisions
T1--09 ▾	History, geographic treatment, biography
T1--0901-T1--0905	**Historical periods**
T1--0901-T1--0905:01	Short term forecasts
T1--0901-T1--0905:02 ▾	Statistics and illustrations
T1--0901-T1--0905:03	Dictionaries, encyclopedias, concordances
T1--0901-T1--0905:05	Serial publications
T1--0901-T1--0905:07 ▾	Museums, collections, exhibits; collecting objects
T1--0901-T1--0905:09 ▾	Archaeology
T1--0901 ▾	*To 499 A.D.
T1--0902 ▾	*6th-15th centuries, 500-1499
T1--0903 ▾	*Modern period, 1500-
T1--0904 ▾	*20th century, 1900-1999
T1--0905 ▾	*21st century, 2000-2099

Figure 8.4. Table 1 --0901-T1--0905 (Historical Periods). *Source*: OCLC

2009). First, let's examine what the asterisks (*) mean in this context. If you click on T1--0901 (To 499 CE), the notes provide this instruction: *Add as instructed under T1--0901–T1--0905. Clicking on "T1--0901–T1--0905" in that instruction takes us to T1--0901–T1--0905 that includes a table of preference and further instructions to add special notation, if needed, to the time period notation. This instruction allows us to add what are essentially standard subdivisions to the time period notation. I would like to return to this in the special notation section below because before we can add special notations, we must add the time period notation!

Since we already have the class number for the eighteenth-century elf folktale book handy (398.2109033), let's dissect it.

398.21 = Tales and lore of paranatural beings of human and semihuman form (elf folktales are included here)

Historical period notation begins with --09, as we can see from Table 1.

The "Modern period, 1500–" is represented by --0903 and we can click on that hyperlink to expand that period's notation (see representation below).

T1--0903 *Modern period, 1500–
   T1--09031 *Sixteenth century, 1500–1599
   T1--09032 *Seventeenth century, 1600–1699
   T1--09033 *Eighteenth century, 1700–1799
   T1--09034 *Nineteenth century, 1800–1899

The eighteenth century is represented by notation --09033. Therefore, we have 398.21 representing elf folklore, and --09033 representing the eighteenth century.

398.21 (Tales and lore of paranatural beings of human and semihuman form)
+
--09033 (eighteenth century)
=
398.2109033 (eighteenth century elf folktales)

A book about the history of fashion in the 1960s would include the class number 391 (Fashion), which requires an extra zero for standard subdivisions. Then we should choose twentieth century, 1900–1999 from Table 1, and finally the notation –009046 (1960–1969):

391 (Fashion)
+
--009046 (1960–1969)
=
391.009046 (Fashion in the 1960s)

Special Notation

As you were exploring Table 1 --08 and --09, you likely noticed a table and table of preference in the notes, like the one at T1—08 (see Figure 8.5).

A key sentence in the notes section is this one: "The subdivisions listed in the add table below are special notation, not standard subdivisions." In

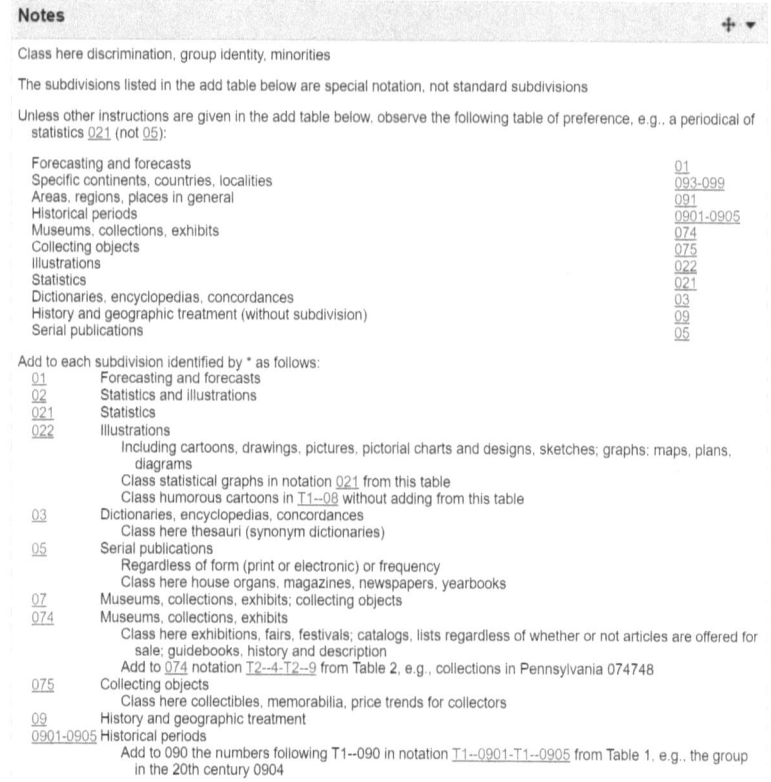

Figure 8.5. Table 1 –08 Notes Area. *Source*: OCLC

other words, despite representing concepts found in the standard subdivisions, they are treated as "special notation" for the purposes of number building. Why would DDC do this? The main reason is that it allows us to include notation from certain areas in Table 1, such as --08 (Groups of people), --0901–0908 (Historical periods), and --093–099 (Specific continents, countries, localities; extraterrestrial worlds), as well as additional notation representing concepts from the standard subdivisions, without having to follow the "only one standard subdivision allowed" rule in DDC. Remember the Table 1 table of preference we explored at the beginning of this chapter? We do not have to worry about that here. Each of the areas listed above has its own table of special notation, as well as a table of preference in case multiple aspects apply.

Let's return to the *Chess for Children* book I used as an example in the "Groups of people" section of this chapter. We determined that the class number for this work is 794.1083, representing both chess (794.1) and children (--083). If we look closely at the beginning of the table in the notes section of --08 (following the table of preference), it says to "Add to each subdivision identified by * as follows:" In other words, we can add the table notation only after the subdivisions that have an asterisk (*). If we go back to "Young people" (--083), we will see that it does, in fact, have an asterisk preceding "Young people." Therefore, we are allowed to add the special notation after --083. If our *Chess for Children* book is heavily illustrated, we can place the "illustrations" (--022) notation from the table at the end of my built class number: 794.1083022.

794.1 (Chess)
+
--083 (Young people from Table 1)
+
--022 (Illustrations from table in the notes section of T1—08)
=
794.1083022 (An illustrated book about chess for children)

We can follow the same process for special notation tables at --0901–0908 (Historical periods) and --093–099 (Specific continents, countries, localities; extraterrestrial worlds). If the example I provided in the Historical periods section above, a book about the history of fashion in the 1960s (391.009046), is actually an encyclopedia of 1960s fashion, we should double-check if the 1960s has an asterisk in front of it (it does) and then locate the notation for encyclopedias in the table found in the notes section of --0901–0908 (Historical periods), which is --03. Like we did above with the illustrated book about chess for children, we take the class number we already built for 1960s fashion (391.009046) and add the notation for encyclopedia (--03).

391 (Fashion)
+
--009046 (1960–1969)
+
--03 (Encyclopedias—from table in the notes section of T1--0901–T1--0905)
=
391.00904603 (An encyclopedia of 1960s fashion)

Finally, the table at --093–099 (Specific continents, countries, localities; extraterrestrial worlds) provides a nice bridge to the next chapter on Table 2, as it requires you add geographic notation from Table 2 first before adding the special notation. Because of the necessity of including notation from Table 2, I will hold off discussing an example for this special notation table until the next chapter. However, please know that the process is still the same as the other special notation tables we discussed in this chapter. Before we move on to Table 2, please practice the many things you have learned in this chapter!

CHAPTER 8 EXERCISES

Answer the following questions using the information provided in this chapter and in WebDewey. Compare your answers to the answers provided in Appendix A.

1. True or False—I can add a standard subdivision to DDC 357 (Mounted forces and warfare).
2. True or False—I can add a standard subdivision to DDC 667.3 (Dyeing and printing) for works about printing alone.
3. True or False—I can add a standard subdivision to DDC 776 (Computer art [Digital art]) if I assign this class number to a work about artistic aspects of virtual reality.

Find the notation in Table 1 (T1--0901–T1--0905) for the following historical periods:

4. 2000–2019
5. Sixteenth century, 1500–1599
6. 999–1 BCE
7. Middle Ages (Medieval period)

Create a DDC number for the following topics using Table 1 notation (<u>underlined</u> in the descriptions on page 71) and explain how you arrived at that number:

Advanced Class Number Building Using Table 1—Part 2   71

8. A book containing <u>research</u> on the manufacture of blouses.
9. An <u>encyclopedia</u> of Atlantis.
10. A <u>serial publication</u> on social psychoanalysis <u>education.</u>
11. Money-saving cooking for <u>married people</u>.
12. A <u>biography</u> of a mathematician.
13. <u>Ancient</u> board games for fun and amusement.

Deconstruct these DDC numbers by explaining the class number, standard subdivision, and/or special notation.

14. 681.114092
15. 791.4509048
16. 641.56110904

NOTE

1. Chan and Mitchell, *Dewey Decimal Classification*, p. 84.

9

Advanced Class Number Building—Including Geographic Places Using Table 2

Now that we have a basic understanding of Table 1, let's move on to Table 2. Table 2 is used primarily to add geographic notation to DDC numbers and, due to the need to cover as many geographic areas as possible, it happens to be the largest table of the six.

The ability to add geographic notation to a DDC number is helpful when classifying works with an emphasis on geographic places; for example, works on the teaching practices in the United States, legal systems in Europe, and gardening in deserts. Note how my geographic examples in the previous sentence are quite different in terms of size and type of location. Table 2 notations include the expected countries, regions, and continents, but also zones (e.g., frigid), socioeconomic regions (e.g., former communist blocs), types of land and landforms (e.g., islands), and ancient places (e.g., Egypt to 640). It even includes extraterrestrial places (such as comets and the Earth's moon), which are unfortunately tacked onto the end of the --9 range of notations that focus on Australasia, Pacific Ocean islands, Atlantic Ocean islands, Arctic islands, and Antarctica.

Before you jump on the Table 2 train for the geographic notation, please double-check the schedules in case the geographic aspect can be included in a different way. For example, Modern western philosophy (190) provides options to class a work by continent or country (191–199), such as the philosophy of the British Isles (192) and the philosophy of Russia (197), without using Table 2 (see representation of 191–199 on page 74).

191–199 Modern western and other noneastern philosophy by continent or country
191 Philosophy of United States and Canada
192 Philosophy of British Isles
193 Philosophy of Germany and Austria
194 Philosophy of France
195 Philosophy of Italy
196 Philosophy of Spain and Portugal
197 Philosophy of Russia
198 Philosophy of Scandinavia and Finland
199 Philosophy in other geographic areas

Other areas of Table 2, such as "Historical periods" (T2--01–T2--5) and Biography (T2--2) rely heavily on Table 1, so I won't go into detail on them here. Follow the instructions in both tables to identify notation on those topics.

Instead, I would like to call your attention to Table 2 notation --1 (Areas, regions, place in general; oceans and seas) and --3 through --9 (Specific continents, countries, localities; extraterrestrial worlds), which I will examine more closely below.

First things first—when building a DDC number using Table 2, you will need to do one of the following:

1. Include --09 after the class number and before the Table 2 notation *unless* . . .
2. The instructions at the class number tell you differently, using the phrase "Add to base number . . . notation . . . from Table 2" or something along those lines.

Let's start with #1. Including the --09 prior to the Table 2 notation stems from the instruction in the Notes at --093–099 (Specific continents, countries, localities; extraterrestrial worlds) in Table 1, about halfway down the page, which reads:

> Add to base number T1--09 notation T2--3–T2--9 from Table 2, e.g., the subject in North America T1--097, in Brazil T1--0981.

Therefore, unless you are instructed otherwise at the class number, you typically include the --09 in front of the Table 2 notation, like so:

307.72 (Rural communities)
+
--09 (From Table 1)
+
--7282 (Belize from Table 2)
=
307.72097282 (Rural communities in the country of Belize)

On the other hand, if the schedules instruct us differently (like in # 2 above), we need to follow those instructions. For example, at 641.593–641.599 (Cooking characteristic of specific continents, countries, localities), if we want to classify a book about cooking in a specific geographic area, we are instructed to

Add to base number 641.59 notation T2--3–T2--9 from Table 2, e.g., Southern cooking (United States) 641.5975

We go through the same motions with Table 2 as we did previously, but without adding --09 before the Table 2 notation. A book about cooking in France (or French cooking), therefore, would be assigned 641.5944.

641.59 (Cooking characteristic of specific geographic environments, ethnic cooking)
+
--44 (France from Table 2)
=
641.5944 (French cooking)

The same can be said of Geography of particular places (913–919). In the Notes area of 913–919 (Geography of and travel in specific continents, countries, localities; extraterrestrial worlds), the following instruction is included:

Add to base number 91 notation T2--3–T2--9 from Table 2, e.g., geography of England 914.2, of Norfolk, England 914.261

To adhere to these instructions, we start with only "91" as the base number, then add Table 2 notation. Let's break down the example provided in the instruction:

91 (Base number for geography of a specific place)
+
--42 (England from Table 2)
=
914.2 (Geography of England)

AREAS, REGIONS, PLACE IN GENERAL; OCEANS AND SEAS (TABLE 2 --1)

Notation from Table 2 beginning with --1 represents "geophysical and conceptually bound but physically scattered areas, such as oceans, temperate zones, and socioeconomic regions."[1] You can see from the Notes area at T2--1 that these areas, regions, etc., are not limited by continent, country, or locality.

Click on each of the hyperlinked options in the hierarchy, specifically T2--11 through T2--17 and T2--18, to expand them. Some expand even further. To give you a better sense of the types of regions included, here is a breakdown:

T2--11–T2--17, Zonal, Physiographic, Socioeconomic Regions

T2--11 Frigid zones
  T2--113 North frigid zone
  T2--116 South frigid zone
T2--12 Temperate zones (Middle latitude zones)
  T2--123 North temperate zone
  T2--126 South temperate zone
  T2--128 Subtropics
T2--13 Torrid zone (Tropics)
T2--14 Land and landforms
  T2--141 Continents
  T2--142 Islands
  T2--143 Elevations

T2--144 Depressions and openings
T2--145 Plane regions
T2--146 Coastal regions and shorelines
T2--148 Soil
T2--15 Regions by type of vegetation
T2--152 Forests
T2--153 Grasslands
T2--154 Deserts
T2--16 Air and water
T2--161 Atmosphere
T2--162 Oceans and seas
T2--163 Atlantic Ocean
T2--164 Pacific Ocean
T2--165 Indian Ocean
T2--167 Antarctic waters
T2--168 Special oceanographic forms and inland seas
T2--169 Fresh and brackish waters
T2--17 Socioeconomic regions
T2--171 Socioeconomic regions by political orientation
T2--172 Socioeconomic regions by degree of economic development
T2--173 Socioeconomic regions by concentration of population
T2--174 Regions where ethnic and national groups predominate
T2--175 Regions where specific languages predominate
T2--176 Regions where specific religions predominate
T2--177 Nations belonging to specific international organizations

T2--18, Other kinds of terrestrial regions

T2--181 Hemispheres
T2--1811 Eastern Hemisphere
T2--1812 Western Hemisphere
T2--1813 Northern Hemisphere
T2--1814 Southern Hemisphere
T2--182 Ocean and sea basins
T2--1821 Atlantic region
T2--1822 Mediterranean region
T2--1823 Pacific region
T2--1824 Indian Ocean region

Under "Zonal, physiographic, socioeconomic regions," for example, there is "Socioeconomic regions" and then "Socioeconomic regions by political orientation." If I am classifying a work on libraries (027) in former communist bloc countries (--1717), there are specific instructions at 027.01–027.09 (Geographic treatment) to build this class number, which *do not* mention the inclusion of --09:

> Add to base number 027.0 notation T2--1-T2--9 from Table 2, e.g., libraries in France 027.044.

Therefore, our class number should be built like this:

027 (Libraries)
+ 0 (as instructed at 027.01-027.09)
+ --1717 (Former communist bloc countries from Table 2)
=
027.01717 (Libraries in former communist bloc countries)

We can use this same pattern to classify works on libraries in the north temperate zone (027.0123), libraries in deserts (027.0154), and libraries on islands (027.0142).

SPECIFIC CONTINENTS, COUNTRIES, LOCALITIES; EXTRATERRESTRIAL WORLDS (T2---3–T2--9)

Places within the ancient world (T2--3), as well as places within the modern world (T2--4–T2--98) and extraterrestrial worlds (T2--99) are covered in the remaining notations for Table 2. The captions for the Ancient World notation are very clear about the time period for the specific place to avoid confusion about whether to use the Ancient or Modern notation (see representation below). Use --31 for works about China up until 420 CE, for example, and --38 for Greece until 323 CE. Beyond those dates, use Table 2 notation for the Modern World for the places listed.

T2--3 Ancient world
   T2--31 China to 420
   T2--32 Egypt to 640

T2--33 Palestine to 70
T2--34 South Asia to 647
T2--35 Mesopotamia to 637 and Iranian Plateau to 637
T2--36 Europe north and west of Italian Peninsula to ca. 499
T2--37 Italian Peninsula to 476 and adjacent territories to 476
T2--38 Greece to 323
T2--39 Other parts of ancient world

The general rule for adding Table 2 notation is to find the main class number, add --09 from Table 1, then add the appropriate geographic place notation from Table 2. If we are classifying a book about table manners in ancient China, we should first find the class number for table manners (395.54), check to see if there are any special instructions (nope!), add --09 (395.5409), and then find the Table 2 notation for China to 420 under the Ancient World (--31).

395.54 (Table manners)
+
--09 (From Table 1)
+
--31 (China to 420, from Table 2)
=
395.540931 (Table manners in ancient China)

Use this same template for modern locations as well (Table 2 --4 through --9). A book about table manners in India would be 395.540954.

395.54 (Table manners)
+
--09 (From Table 1)
+
--54 (India, from Table 2)
=
395.540954 (Table manners in India)

Remember: Unless there are instructions in the schedules to the contrary, the general rule for adding Table 2 notation is: **base class number + --09 (Table 1) + Table 2 notation**.

TRAVEL GUIDEBOOKS

Travel guidebooks for tourists also incorporate Table 2 notation, but in an interesting way. The Manual at 913-919 says to:

1) Start at 913–919,
2) find the geographic place that is the subject of the guidebook in that range, but also in Table 2,
3) and then add --04 from the table at 913–919.

Let's use a travel guidebook for New York City as an example.

The range of 913–919 is largely organized by continent. New York City is on the North American continent, so choose 917—"Geography of and travel in North America." There is an entry, 917.4–917.9 for "Geography of and travel in specific states of United States," and its Notes area says,

> Add to base number 91 notation T2--74–T2--79 from Table 2, e.g., geography of and travel in California 917.94; then add further as instructed under 913–919, e.g., travel in California 917.9404, travel in California in 2001 917.940454.

This means that we need to find notation for New York City in Table 2 and place it after a base number of 91. New York (City) is --7471 in Table 2, and adding that to the end of 91 makes 917.471.

Since the initial instructions at 913–919 say to add --04 to the end of the class number to denote a travel guidebook, we need to do that as well: **917.47104**.

Figure 9.1. New York City Travel Guidebook. *Source*: Lauren Enjeti

91 (Base notation for geography and travel)
+
--7471 (New York City from Table 2)
+
--04 (Notation for travel guidebooks, from the table at 913–919)
=
917.47104 (New York City travel guidebook for tourists)

Advanced Class Number Building—Including Geographic Places Using Table 2

As I mentioned previously, you have to be on the lookout for these special cases.

"SPECIAL NOTATION" FROM TABLE 1 (T1--093–T1--099)

Finally, I want to point out an important table in Table 1 (T1--093–T1--099) that is similar to the one we explored at the end of Chapter 8 and can be used in addition to the Table 2 notation. Go to T1--093–T1--099 in Table 1 to see what is captured in Figure 9.2.

In a nutshell, this entry is saying you can add certain "standard subdivision-like" notations to a class number with Table 2 geographic notation. Once again, note the statement, "The subdivisions listed in the add table below are special notation, not standard subdivisions." After the table of preference, we are provided with the instruction:

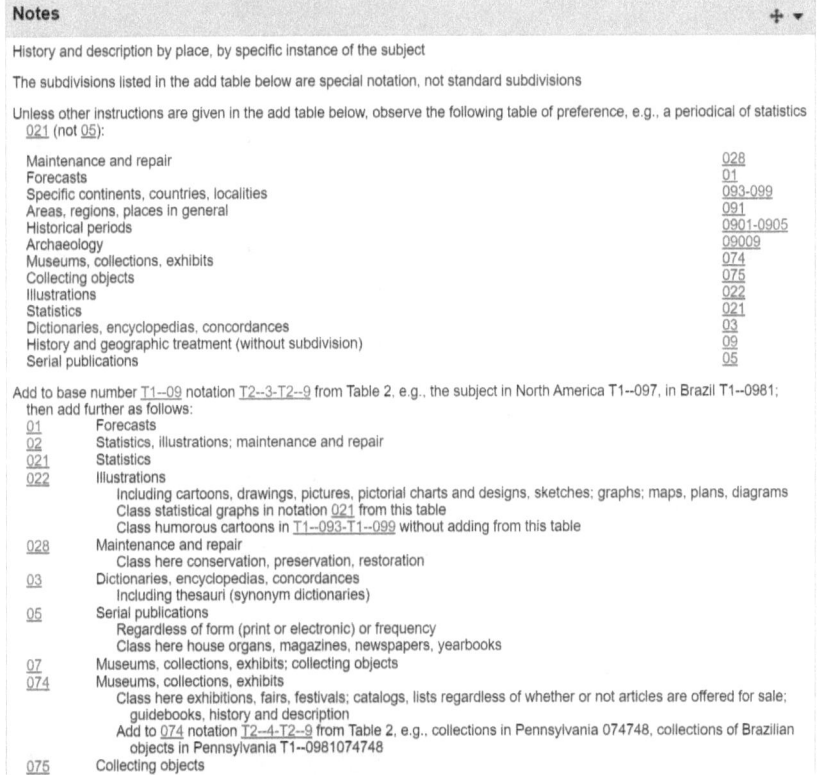

Figure 9.2. Notes at T1--093-T1--099. *Source:* OCLC

Add to base number T1--09 notation T2--3–T2--9 from Table 2, e.g., the subject in North America T1--097, in Brazil T1--0981; then add further as follows.

Many of the Table 1 standard subdivisions are here, and we can place one of them after the geographic notation from Table 2, if it applies and there is nothing in the schedules that says you cannot. Going back to our table manners in India example, 395.540954, if this work is a serial publication on this topic, we can add the serial publications "special notation" (--05) from the add table to the end of the class number: **395.54095405**.

395.54 (Table manners)
+
--09 (From Table 1)
+
--54 (India, from Table 2)
+
--05 (Serial publications "special notation" from Table 1)
=
395.54095405 (Serial publication on table manners in India)

Once again, this process may produce a DDC number far longer than needed or what will fit comfortably on a spine label, so don't feel like you must add the special notation unless this level of specificity is needed. Nonetheless, the special notation provides a "loophole" that allows the inclusion of multiple table notations if that is desired.

Resources that emphasize geographic location are popular, so having a mechanism to include this information in the DDC number can be helpful. Table 2 is the most common source of geographic notation, but don't forget that some class numbers can incorporate geographic information without the aid of Table 2, like my Modern Western Philosophy—190—example at the beginning of this chapter. The next chapter will cover Table 3, which takes us into the realm of literature.

CHAPTER 9 EXERCISES

Answer the following questions using the information provided in this chapter and in WebDewey. Compare your answers to the answers provided in Appendix A.

1. True or False—Geography can only be noted by using Table 2.
2. True or False—Table 2 allows you to include notation representing socioeconomic regions by political orientation.
3. True or False—I suggest using any and all tables and special notations that you can to create the longest possible call number.

Find the Table 2 notation for the following geographic places, either by browsing Table 2 or using the Relative Index:

4. Algeria
5. South Georgia and South Sandwich Islands
6. The planet Jupiter
7. Iceland
8. Southern Hemisphere

Create a DDC number for the following works using either Table 2 or a combination of Table 1 and Table 2:

9. A book on cooking brunch in the United States.
10. A travel guidebook for Brazil.
11. A history of Ancient Greece during the Hellenistic period, 323–146 BCE
12. A book on sports in Central America
13. A book on the geography of Southeast Asia.
14. A book on printmaking in the Mariana Islands.

NOTE

1. Chan and Mitchell, *Dewey Decimal Classification*, p. 100.

10

Advanced Class Number Building Using Table 3—Subdivisions for the Arts, for Individual Literatures, for Specific Literary Forms

Table 3 is titled "Subdivisions for the Arts, for Individual Literatures, for Specific Literary Forms," but contains no content. It is more accurate to say that Table 3 is a series of sub-tables (3A, 3B, and 3C) that apply to different situations, which I will explain more about momentarily. The most important thing to remember about using the Table 3 sub-tables is that they apply primarily to class numbers in the 800s (Literature), so we will be spending quite a bit of this chapter in that class.

Of all the Dewey classes, the 800 class is one of the most faceted, meaning that each part of the class number stems from different categories of notation, such as language, form, and time period. We have seen this plenty of times in previous chapters when building class numbers from the schedule text or the other tables, but the 800s rely heavily on Table 3 sub-tables for their existence. For example, an anthology of English Romanticism literature would be assigned class number 820.80145, which includes a base number "82" representing English literature, the "080" from Table 3B representing collections of literary texts in more than one form, and then "145" from Table 3C representing Romanticism (see Figure 10.1).

In this chapter, I will start by discussing Table 3A, which provides subdivisions for literary works by or about *individual authors*. Then we will explore Tables 3B and 3C, which are used when classifying literary works by or about *more than one author*. Finally, I will explain how to classify

An anthology of English Romanticism literature

$$\underline{8\,2}\underline{0}.\underline{80}\underline{1}\underline{45}$$

English lit. Table 3B –   Table 3C – Romanticism
              Collections of literary
              texts in more than
              one form

Figure 10.1. Anthology of English Romanticism Literature. *Source:* Karen Snow

general collections of world literature that feature two or more languages, particularly using class number 808.

My goal with this chapter and Chapter 11 is to introduce you to Tables 3–6 and their uses, but not go into great depth. If you need more in-depth guidance on DDC number building using these tables, I recommend consulting some of the sources I list in Chapter 12, especially Chan and Mitchell (2003) and Satija and Kyrios (2023).

TABLE 3A, SUBDIVISIONS FOR WORKS BY OR ABOUT INDIVIDUAL AUTHORS

Table 3A is probably the most straightforward of the Table 3 sub-tables. Use this table to build a DDC number for works *by* or *about* an individual author. Yes, you read that right—class together not only works by an individual author, but also works about the author and their associated works, which can be fantastic or frustrating, depending on your point of view. For example, *Great Expectations*, a novel by Charles Dickens; a biography of Charles Dickens; and a criticism of *Great Expectations* should be assigned the same DDC number: 823.8. And that includes translations, too!

The opportunities DDC provides to bring together literary works by and about an author do not always translate into library practice. It is not uncommon for libraries that use DDC to place all biographies in one section, regardless of the occupation or area of influence of the biography subject, as I mentioned back in Chapter 8 (advanced DDC number building using Table 1). The same can be said of fiction works, with many libraries choosing to place fiction by individual authors in a general "Fiction" section or organized by genre—mystery, science fiction, romance, etc. Please keep this in mind as you read this chapter.

With that said, how about we continue with the Dickens example to see how Table 3A works?

If we click on Table 3A, we encounter a very busy Notes area, so let me break this down for you in simple terms. Your literature class number for individual authors is composed of the following (generally speaking):

language + form + time period = class number for literary work

That's it. I will expand upon this formula in the following sections.

1) In which language did the author primarily write?

The first step in creating a class number for an individual author is to determine the language of the work. To do this, we *do not* start at Table 3A. Find the language in the 810–890 class number range while noting that American (810) and British (820) English have separate class numbers:

810 American literature in English
820 English & Old English literatures
830 German & related literatures
840 French & related literatures
850 Italian, Romanian & related literatures
860 Spanish, Portuguese, Galician literatures
870 Latin & Italic literatures
880 Classical & modern Greek literatures
890 Other literatures

The 800s suffer from the bias toward Western languages, cultures, history, etc., that I mentioned in the Preface, as evidenced by the number of non-European languages crammed into 890—Other literatures. Browse 890 or use the WebDewey search function to find a language not listed at the division level of the 800s.

If we stick with the Charles Dickens example, we should choose 820 (English & Old English literatures) because Dickens was an author who wrote in English and lived in England. One thing to keep in mind in this process is that it is just the first two numbers in the class number that represent literature and the language (82 in our Dickens example), not the entire three digits. To determine the third digit, we need to ask...

2) In what literary form is the work?

Next, we need to establish the literary form of the work. To answer this question, we need to leave the 800s and go to Table 3A, which provides the literary forms to populate the third digit in our class number (see reproduction of Specific forms at T3A--1 through T3A--8 below).

T3A--1–T3A--8 Specific forms
   T3A--1 Poetry
   T3A--2 Drama
   T3A--3 Fiction
   T3A--4 Essays
   T3A--5 Speeches
   T3A--6 Letters
   T3A--8 Miscellaneous writings

If there are multiple literary forms present in the work, Table 3A provides a table of preference in the Notes area so you can determine which form to choose. Otherwise, choose the literary form that applies to the work you are classifying. *Great Expectations* by Charles Dickens is a fiction novel, which is covered in T3A--3 (Fiction) along with novelettes and short stories. Therefore, we add "3" (Fiction) to the "82" (English literature) from the last step, making our class number 823 (English fiction).

3) In which time period did the author write?

Finally, we need to include notation for time period in the class number. To answer this question, we need to go *back* to 810–890 in the schedules (insert sound of whiplash). Since we already determined that 820 is the class number area we need for *Great Expectations*, let's go back there. To locate the time periods, we need to click on 821–828—Subdivisions for specific forms of English literature.

Once you click on the hyperlinked 821–828, you will see a list of time periods alongside some strange-looking class numbers. Let's zoom in on the entries at the beginning that represent English authors in England (as opposed to Ireland and Australia, for example)—see reproduction below.

821–828 Subdivisions for specific forms of English literature
    821–828:1 Early English period, 1066–1400
    821–828:2 1400–1558
    821–828:3 Elizabethan period, 1558–1625
    821–828:4 1625–1702
    821–828:5 Queen Anne period, 1702–1745
    821–828:6 1745–1799
    821–828:7 1800–1837
    821–828:8 Victorian period, 1837–1899
    821–828:9 1900–

The colon (:) plus number at the end of the 821–828 range of numbers does *not* mean that you add a colon and number to your existing class number. Instead, it means the number after the colon, representing a particular time period, is added to the class number we have already built (which, to refresh your memory, is 823). The table in the Notes area at 821–828 includes the Period Table for English, which provides the number we need to add to our class number (see Figure 10.2).

If you are not familiar with the author of the work you are classifying, this part will be more challenging. A quick search of Charles Dickens reveals that he lived from 1812 until 1870, which overlaps two periods on the table: "7" representing 1800–1837, and "8" representing the Victorian period of 1837–1899. To determine which to choose, we should establish the time period in which the author was most prolific. For Dickens, that would be the latter period of 1837–1899 (as I learned from exploring his publishing history online). Place the "8" representing 1837–1899 at the end of the class number we have been building, 823, to make 823.8. Therefore, this confirms our earlier assignment of 823.8 to *Great Expectations* and all other works by and about Dickens.

```
Notes

Except for modifications shown under specific entries, add to base number 82 as instructed at beginning of T3--0, e.g., a
collection of English literature 820.8

Use the following period table for literature from all countries and continents except North America, South America, Hawaii,
and associated islands; for comprehensive works on literature in English language

PERIOD TABLE FOR ENGLISH
    1           Early English period, 1066-1400
                    Class here medieval period
    2           1400-1558
    3           Elizabethan period, 1558-1625
                    Class here 16th century; Renaissance and Jacobean periods
                    For 1500-1558, the pre-Elizabethan part of the Renaissance, see notation 2 from this table
    4           1625-1702
                    Class here Caroline and Restoration periods
    5           Queen Anne period, 1702-1745
                    Class here 18th century
                    For 1700-1702, see notation 4 from this table
                    For 1745-1799, see notation 6 from this table
    6           1745-1799
    7           1800-1837
                    Class here romantic period
    8           Victorian period, 1837-1899
                    Class here 19th century
                    For 1800-1837, see notation 7 from this table
    9           1900-
    91          1900-1999
    912         1900-1945
    914         1945-1999
    92          2000-
```

Figure 10.2.   Notes Area of 821-828. *Source*: OCLC

82 (English literature from 810–890 in the schedules)

+

3 (Fiction from Table 3A)

+

8 (Victorian period, 1837–1899, from the table at 821–828)

=

823.8 (Fiction works by Charles Dickens)

This class number applies equally to Dickens and any other English author of the Victorian era, regardless of the books' topic. For this reason, fiction works being classified as literature and not by subject can be frustrating and/or confusing when using DDC.

Cutter numbers, mentioned in Chapter 1 of this book, can be very helpful for keeping books by the same author together on the shelf, but not as helpful for works *about* an author that have the same class number and a different author (for example, a biography of Charles Dickens by Jack Smith). This is an issue that individual libraries must address in their local policies if they choose to follow DDC closely rather than put biographies in a separate section.

Additionally, organizing the fiction works by genre can also help you avoid a mass of books with the same class number and Cutter number. The class numbers and Cutter numbers would be the same, but works could be placed in the genres designated by the library (e.g., romance, mystery, etc.) and therefore broken up a bit. Unfortunately, DDC does not allow us to create class numbers that include genre information for literary works by and about individual authors—only for literary works by two or more authors, as we will see very shortly when we discuss Table 3B. Once again, local policy will need to dictate the use (or non-use) of fiction genres.

There are, of course, exceptions to all of the above. There are options to add further notation to "Miscellaneous writings" (T3A--8), which includes specific form notation for diaries, riddles, epigrams, quotations, and many others. Create the class number normally like we did above, then add the "miscellaneous" notation from the table in the Notes area of T3A--81–T3A--89 (for example, published diaries of Charles Dickens would be assigned **823.803**). In addition, William Shakespeare is a big exception as he has his very own class number, 822.33, as well as options out the wazoo for subarranging (just go to 822.33 and you will see what I mean). This includes subarrangement by complete works and individual works—a template that can be modified for other prolific authors if a library so chooses.

Now that we have covered the basics of Table 3A, let's move on to Tables 3B and 3C.

TABLE 3B—SUBDIVISIONS FOR WORKS BY OR ABOUT MORE THAN ONE AUTHOR AND TABLE 3C— ADDITIONAL NOTATION FOR ARTS AND LITERATURE

I will discuss Table 3B and 3C together as they are closely associated; in fact, there may be instances when you will use both in tandem. As the title of Table 3B states, you will use this table if you are classifying works by or about *more than one author*. The Manual entry for Table 3B is quite helpful, and it includes two flow charts (linked to at the bottom of the Notes area of Manual entry T3B--0) that help you make decisions on how to proceed: one flow chart is for "Works by or about more than one author" and the other is for "notation T3B--8 Miscellaneous writings." The flow chart for "Works by or about more than one author" can be found in Appendix B of this book for easy reference.

Tables 3B and 3C can be used to construct class numbers for collections (--08 from Table 3B), as well as criticisms (--09 from, Table 3B) of literature in more than one form (fiction, drama, etc.) or in only one form.

The construction of class numbers using 3B and 3C depends heavily upon what information you want to include in the class number. Satija and Kyrios write that Tables 3B and 3C require "different paths for number building depending on the presence of absence of facets such as form, period, standard subdivisions, themes, and people."[1] Therefore, a class number can be as simple as 821 for a collection of English poetry, or as complex as 821.914080324253 for collections of later-twentieth-century English-language poetry about travel in Lincolnshire (holy moly).

Literary Collections of One Form

Regardless of the many facets we are able to include, always start with language, like we did with Table 3A. This is confirmed in the Notes area of Table 3B, which has a list of eight steps with instructions on how to build a class number. To illustrate how this works, let's walk through a straightforward example: an anthology of short stories by twentieth century American authors, a literary work of only one form (short stories), but also includes language (American English) and time period (twentieth century) information.

Like with Table 3A, we are told at Table 3B to "Look in the schedule 810–890 to find the base number for the language." American literature in English is represented by DDC 810, and we focus on the first two digits of that class number: **81**.

Notation for Form

Next, we head back to Table 3B to determine the literary form. Table 3B seems very similar to Table 3A in this area, but look closer and you will see some differences. Interestingly, short stories, which are included in the Fiction area (--3) in Table 3A, are not mentioned in the Fiction area of Table 3B. Instead, we need to dig deeper into T3B--3 (Fiction), expanding the section titled "Fiction of specific scope and kinds." It is there that we find T3B--301 (Short stories):

T3B--301–T3B--308 Fiction of specific scope and kinds
T3B--301 *Short stories
T3B--308 Specific kinds of fiction

There are a few items to which I want to draw your attention. The first is the presence of the asterisk (*) next to "Short stories." If we look in the Notes area, it says, "Add to each subdivision identified by * as instructed under T3B--102–T3B--107, e.g., collections of short stories dealing with travel T3B--3010832." This instruction provides helpful guidance in case we want to specify a particular topic or theme of the short story collection, like travel.

Another item I want to point out is the "Specific kinds of fiction" section at T3B--308, something not included in Table 3A (see reproduction below). Expanding this section reveals that we can include notation for genre, such as romance fiction, historical fiction, and science fiction (yay!), but only for works by or about more than one author, not individual authors (boo!).

T3B--308 Specific kinds of fiction
   T3B--3081 *Historical and period fiction
   T3B--3082 *Autobiographical and biographical fiction
   T3B--3083 *Psychological, realistic, sociological fiction
   T3B--3085 *Love and romance
   T3B--3087 *Adventure fiction

To put this to use, we could create a class number for a collection of romance fiction by American authors by taking 81 (American literature in English) and adding --3085 (Love and romance from Table 3B): **813.085**. If there are multiple kinds of fiction included in the collection you are classifying, there is a table of preference at T3B--308 (Specific kinds of fiction). For example, a historical romance fiction collection would include only the notation for "Historical and period fiction" (--3081) and not "Love and romance" (--0385) because "Historical and period fiction" is higher up in the table of preference.

Let's get back to our example of an anthology of short stories by 20th century American authors. If we don't want to emphasize the genre, we can simply add the notation for short stories (--301) to our base number of 81 (American literature in English) to create the class number **813.01**. But we're not done. This is an anthology of short stories by twentieth century American authors; we still need to add the time period aspect, if possible, to our class number.

Notation for Time Period

To add the time period notation, we are told in the Notes area of Table 3B that we should "follow the instructions in the table under T3B--102–T3B--107 in Table 3B." Since "Short stories" has an asterisk (*) next to it, we can add further notation representing time period: 0801–0809 (Specific periods). Here we are told to "Add to 080 notation from the period table for the specific literature, e.g., Elizabethan period of English literature 0803, collections of English sonnets of the Elizabethan period 821.0420803." The "period table" mentioned in this instruction refers to the period tables found in each literature in 810–890. Since we have a work of American literature, we need to return to 810 (American literature in English) <whiplash> and consult the period table found at 811–818 (Subdivisions for specific forms of American literature in English). The twentieth century is covered at 1900–1999, which is represented by "5." To recap, we have:

81 (American literature)
+
--301 (Short stories from Table 3B)
+
--080 (Notation representing specific time periods from T3B--102-T3B--107 in Table 3B)
+
5 (1900-1999 from the period table at 810)
=

813.010805 (Anthology of short stories by twentieth-century American authors)

TABLE 3C NOTATION FOR THEMES, SUBJECTS, STYLE, MOOD, VIEWPOINT, OR PERSONS

Finally, Table 3C provides additional notation for arts and literature, such as themes and subjects (e.g., the supernatural, holidays); elements (e.g., narrative, plot); qualities of style, mood, or viewpoint (e.g., irony, realism, modernism); and specific kinds of persons (e.g., young people, lesbians), in that order of preference. Table 3C does not even need to be used through Table 3B, as the Notes area of Table 3B clarifies:

> Notation from Table 3C is never used alone, but may be used where instructed in Table 3B, 398.2–398.3, 659.1, 700.4, 741.5, 791.4, 794.84, 808–809.

Note that, in addition to Table 3B, we can use Table 3C with the specified class numbers. For example, 794.84 (Specific aspects of electronic games) encourages the use of Table 3C to emphasize themes and subjects in electronic games, such as electronic games that feature legendary beings. The instructions state:

> Add to base number 794.84 the numbers following T3C--3 in notation T3C--32–T3C--39 from Table 3C

Therefore, we use 794.84 as the base number and then add notation for legendary being from Table 3C (--375) but minus the initial "3."

794.84 (Specific aspects of electronic games)
+
--75 (Legendary beings from Table 3C, the numbers following --3, as instructed)
=
794.8475 (Electronic games featuring legendary beings)

Otherwise, we can use Table 3B as a jumping-off point to add Table 3C notation, with the understanding that (generally speaking) we cannot include both a time period and Table 3C "theme" notation in a class number, so we would have to choose which one to include if both are present. A work on sexual themes in Victorian literature, for example, can include the time period aspect (Victorian), but not the theme (sex).

To illustrate usage of Table 3C through Table 3B, let's try another example: a collection of American poetry with religious themes.

Setting Table 3C aside for a moment, we can start this class number as we have the entire chapter: by going to the 800 literature class and finding American literature in English: 810. We can also see by browsing through 810 that "American poetry in English" is classed at 811, which combines 810 with "1" from Table 3B representing "poetry." So far, so good, but there is one more step before we can add notation for "religious themes" to complete the class number.

At T3B--102–T3B--107 (which you can find by clicking on T3B--1 (Poetry) and locating "Specific kinds of poetry"), locate the entry for "Collections of literary texts" and click on it. We need to pay attention to the instruction for "Literature displaying specific features, or emphasizing subjects, or for and by groups of people" (T3B--102–T3B--107:081–089). In this Notes area, we are told:

> Add to 08 notation T3C--1–T3C--9 from Table 3C, e.g., collections dealing with love 083543, collections of English sonnets dealing with love 821.042083543

This is a long way of saying that, before we can include the Table 3C notation, we must include --08 to signify that we have a collection of poetry that has specific features, emphasizes a subject, or is for/by groups of people. Therefore, add --08 to 811 to create 811.08, representing a collection of American poetry that emphasizes a particular theme.

Finally, we can consult Table 3C for the "religious themes" notation. Remember that Table 3C contains notation representing themes and subjects, as well as many other topics (see Figure 10.3).

If we drill down into T3C--3—Arts and literature dealing with specific themes and subjects, there are several options, one of which is "Philosophic and abstract themes" at T3C--38. Click on it to see further options (reproduced below).

T3C--38 Philosophic and abstract themes
   T3C--382 Religious themes
   T3C--384 Philosophic themes

T3C--0 Table 3C. Additional Notation for Arts and Literature

T3C--0	Table 3C. Additional Notation for Arts and Literature
T3C--001-T3C--007	Standard subdivisions
T3C--[008]	Groups of people
T3C--009	History and geographic treatment
T3C--01-T3C--09	Specific periods
T3C--1	Arts and literature displaying specific qualities of style, mood, viewpoint
T3C--2	Literature displaying specific elements
T3C--3	Arts and literature dealing with specific themes and subjects
T3C--4	Literature emphasizing subjects
T3C--8-T3C--9	Literature for and by groups of people

Figure 10.3. Table 3C – Additional Notation for Arts and Literature. *Source*: OCLC

"Religious themes" is represented by --382. We could get even *more* specific if a particular religion (Judaism = --38296) or a specific aspect (Hell = --382023) was emphasized, but that is not the case here. Therefore, our class number for a collection of American poetry with religious themes is: **811.08382**.

81 (American literature)
+
--1 (Poetry from Table 3B)
+
--08 (Notation from Table 3B indicating that subject, theme, etc. notation from Table 3C is coming next)
+
--382 (Religious themes from Table 3C)
=
811.08382 (Collection of American poetry with religious themes)

There are ways to include other facets, such as time period, geographic place, and subjects, that provide the opportunity to create truly breathtaking class numbers, like this one that takes advantage of most of the DDC tables:

82 (English literature)
+
--09 (History, description, critical appraisal from Table 3B)
+
--32 (Literature dealing with places from Table 3C)
+
--415 (Ireland from Table 2)
+
--09031 (sixteenth century, 1500–1599 from Table 1)
=

820.93241509031 (An anthology of sixteenth-century British literature on Ireland)

The combination of notations you can include in a literature class number using Tables 3B and 3C are truly staggering and, once again, I encourage you to consult Chan and Mitchell (2003) in particular (see citation in Chapter 12) to learn more about these constructions.

GENERAL COLLECTIONS OF LITERARY TEXTS IN MORE THAN TWO LITERATURES

Our focus thus far in this chapter has been on creating class numbers for literary works by or about one author, and literary works by or about multiple authors who write in one language. General collections or criticisms of literary works that are not limited to one language should be classed in 800–809, except for collections that contain texts in more than two languages from the same language family (for example, collection of French, Italian, and Spanish literatures—all Romance languages).

The class number 808.8 represents "Collections of literary texts from more than two literatures" and is therefore commonly used to classify general anthologies of world literature. In fact, due to the complexities of classifying in the 800 class and using the Table 3 sub-tables, the use of the class 808 only for any collection of literary texts from more than two literatures is a popular choice if we look at the number of texts at 808 in LibraryThing's Melvil Decimal System widget: https://www.librarything.com/mds/808. However, DDC has plenty of options for creating greater specificity.

ADDING FORM, THEMES/PERSONS, AND TIME PERIOD

Returning to 808.8, we are allowed to build on this base number if we want to add form, time period, or themes/persons. For instance, a collection of world drama should be assigned 808.82 (--2 representing drama from Table 3B), but we can go even further into Table 3B and assign notation for "tragedy" instead of "drama" generally using --20512: **808.820512 (a collection of world tragedies)**. We can use Table 3C to include notation representing specific themes or persons, such as a collection of literature that features Count Dracula—808.80351.

> 808.80 (Base number for collections of literature displaying specific features—808.801–808.803)
> +
> --351 (Specific persons from Table 3C, including Count Dracula)
> =
> **808.80351 (A collection of literature that features Count Dracula)**

Adding time period notation can also be useful if you have a collection of literature from a specific time period, such as the twentieth century, for example. Once again, at 808.8, there is an option to choose "Collections from specific periods" at 808.8001–808.8005. The instruction in the Notes area here says:

> Add to base number 808.800 the numbers following T1--090 in notation T1--0901–T1--0905 from Table 1, e.g., collections of 18th century literature 808.80033.

Therefore, to add time period, we need to consult Table 1. The Table 1 notation for the twentieth century is --0904, and the instruction above says to add the numbers following --090 (so, in this case "4") to 808.800, making 808.8004.

808.800 (Base number for collections of literary texts from more than two literatures by specific time period)
+
--4 (Number from --0904 in Table 1 representing the twentieth century)
=

808.8004 (A collection of twentieth-century literary texts from more than two literatures)

The Table 3 sub-tables and the 800 class provide many options and opportunities to build class numbers for literary works, depending on your library's needs. Remember: Table 3A = literary works by or about *individual authors*. Tables 3B and 3C = literary works by or about *more than one author*.

The next chapter will wrap up our discussion of DDC tables by exploring Tables 4, 5, and 6.

CHAPTER 10 EXERCISES

Answer the following questions using the information provided in this chapter and in WebDewey. Compare your answers to the answers provided in Appendix A.

1. According to Table 3A, which notation represents Fiction? What about Miscellaneous writings?
2. According to Table 3B, which notation represents Humor and satire? What about Diaries, journals, notebooks, reminiscences?
3. According to Table 3C, which notation represents literature displaying stream of consciousness? What about Arts and literature dealing with plants?

Use Table 3A to create a class number for the following works:

4. The novel *Frankenstein*, by English author Mary Shelley (1797–1851).
5. *If It Bleeds*, a collection of short stories by American author Stephen King (1947–).

6. *Mord auf Raten*, a novel by German author Andreas Franz (1954--2011).
7. *Bad Feminist*, a book of essays by American author Roxane Gay (1974–).
8. *Call Us What We Carry*, a book of poems by American poet Amanda Gorman (1998–).
9. A collection of plays by Irish playwright, poet, and author Oscar Wilde (1854–1900).

Use Tables 3B (and potentially Table 3C) to a create a class number for the following works.

10. A collection of essays by Spanish authors.
11. An anthology of English ghost stories.
12. A collection of English ballads from the Queen Anne period.
13. An anthology of French drama for children.
14. An American collection of humor and satire that has a "holiday" theme.

Use Table 3C to create a class number for the following works:

15. Electronic games featuring animals.
16. A collection of literature that features magic and witchcraft.
17. A work on nontraditional viewpoints in the arts.

NOTE

1. Kyrios, A., and Satija, M. P. (2023). *A Handbook of History, Theory and Practice of the Dewey Decimal Classification System.* Facet Publishing, p. 105.

11

Advanced Class Number Building Using Tables 4–6—Languages and Ethnic and National Groups

In this final chapter on DDC tables, we will explore Table 4—Subdivisions of Individual Languages and Language Families, Table 5—Ethnic and National Groups, and Table 6—Languages. First, I will cover Tables 4 and 6 in one section due to their similar focus: languages. Then we will discuss the use of Table 5 to include notation for ethnic and national groups.

TABLE 4 AND TABLE 6

Tables 4 (Subdivisions of Individual Languages and Language Families) and 6 (Languages) are often discussed together, for good reason—both focus on languages. Like Table 3's focus on the 800 (Literature) class, Table 4 (Subdivisions of Individual Languages and Language Families) predominantly supports number building in the 400 (Language) class. Table 4 is particularly useful for classifying language dictionaries, works on grammar, or works on the etymology of words in a language.

Table 6 (Languages) not only provides additional notation in support of Table 4; it also can be used in many areas of the schedules beyond the 400 class (unlike Table 4), assuming there are explicit instructions to do so. For example, a French-language Bible should be assigned the class number 220.541, which combines the base number for Bible versions in languages other than English (220.5) with Table 6 notation for the French language (--41).

Chapter 11

Like with all the tables, it is critical to follow the instructions provided in Tables 4 and 6, and not use any of the table notation on its own—you must start with a class or base number from the schedules and add table notation when appropriate and/or instructed to do so.

Digging into Table 4

Some of Table 4 looks very similar to the standard subdivisions in Table 1, but there are other aspects unique to Table 4. T4--1–T4--5, which provides notation for the description and analysis of the standard form of the language, includes more specific notation (that can be expanded even further) for writing systems, phonology, phonetics, etymology, dictionaries, and grammar (see Figure 11.1).

Many of the 400 class numbers are already built using Table 4, saving us a lot of time and effort; for example, 423, the class number for English-language dictionaries, is composed of the base number for English & Old English Languages (42) plus notation representing dictionaries from Table 4 (--3). Looking at the structure of 421–428 (the subdivisions of English), for example, it clearly mirrors that of Table 4 (421–428 reproduced on page 105).

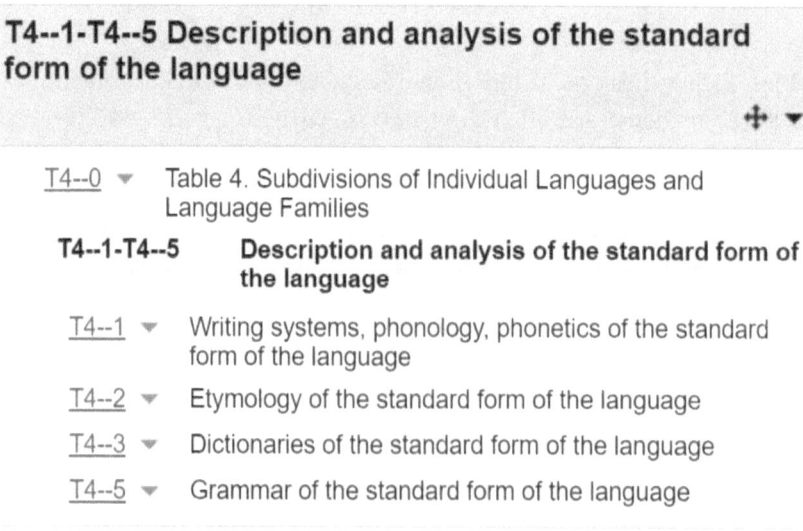

Figure 11.1. Table 4 - T4--1-T4--5 (Description and Analysis of the Standard Form of the Language). *Source*: OCLC

Advanced Class Number Building Using Tables 4–6 105

421–428 Subdivisions of English
421 Writing system, phonology, phonetics of standard English
422 Etymology of standard English
423 Dictionaries of standard English
[424] [Unassigned]
425 Grammar of standard English
[426] [Unassigned]
427 Historical and geographic variations, modern nongeographic variations of English
428 Standard English usage (Prescriptive linguistics)

Just like with other DDC tables, start with the base language number from the schedules, then add notation from Table 4, and (if needed) standard subdivisions from Table 1.

The main languages mentioned in 420–480 are a clear indication of the Western bias in DDC, as 490 is extremely crowded with non-Western-centric languages, including Japanese, Russian, and Arabic languages. These numbers will necessarily be longer but will still follow the same pattern for number building I mentioned above. For example, Japanese-language dictionaries are classed at 495.63.

495.6 (Japanese language)
+
--3 (Dictionaries from Table 4)
=
495.63 (Japanese-language dictionary)

What I discussed above applies to works in one language. Works that contain more than one language will need an assist from Table 6 to build the class number. However, that is not all Table 6 can provide.

What's Going on With Table 6?

On the surface Table 6 seems odd and redundant, containing entries for the languages we have already seen in Table 4 (see reproduction on page 106).

T6--0 Table 6. Languages
  T6--1–T6--9 Languages
   T6--1 Indo-European languages
   T6--2–T6--8 Specific Indo-European languages other than east Indo-European languages and Celtic languages
   T6--9 Other languages

However, as I mentioned in the introduction to this chapter, Table 6 provides language notation if we want to include the language aspect of a subject (like the French-language Bible), something we cannot do with Table 4. Keep in mind that we can add Table 6 notation only when explicitly instructed in the schedules and not wherever we want. Some examples of class numbers that have instructions for using Table 6 are:

031–039—General encyclopedic works in specific languages and language families
Example: 036 (base number for general encyclopedic works in a specific language) + --9 (Portuguese from Table 6) = **036.9 (Portuguese-language encyclopedias)**
398.204—Folk literature by language
Example: 398.204 (base number for folk literature by language) + --41 (French from Table 6) = **398.20441 (folktales from French-speaking areas of the world)**
372.652–372.659—Specific foreign, official, second languages within "Primary education (Elementary education)"
Example: 372.65 (base number for second languages in elementary education) + --21 (English from Table 6) = **372.6521 (English as a second language in elementary education)**

Bilingual Dictionaries

Classifying dictionaries containing more than one language is a little more complex. These types of dictionaries are fairly common; they include translations from one language into another, as well as definitions. However, some bilingual dictionaries have the entry words in only one language, while others have entry words in both languages. The Table 4 entry for bilingual dictionaries (T4--32–T4--39) has the following instruction in the Notes area on what to do.

Add to base number T4--3 notation T6--2–T6--9 from Table 6, e.g., dictionaries of the language and English T4--321, dictionary of French and English 443.21.

A bilingual dictionary with entry words in only one language is classed with that language, e.g., an English-French dictionary 423.41. A bilingual dictionary with entry words in both languages aimed at speakers of only one of the languages is classed with the other language, e.g., a bilingual dictionary with entry words in French and English but with introduction and explanatory apparatus only in French is classed with English in 423.41. A bilingual dictionary with entry words in both languages aimed at speakers of both languages is classed with the language coming later in 420–490, e.g., French-German, German-French dictionaries 443.31.

According to this Notes area, we need to use both Table 4 and Table 6 to construct a class number for bilingual dictionaries. The basic formula is this:

Class number for the primary language in the 400s, minus the final zero if there is one
+ --3 (Dictionaries from Table 4)
+ notation for the second language from Table 6

The "primary" language is generally determined by identifying which language has entry words first; the "second" language provides the meaning of the entry words. For example, if I am classifying an English-Polish dictionary with the entry words in English and the meaning of those words in Polish, English is the primary language and Polish is the secondary language. If we continue with this example, we need to find English in the 400s (420) and remove the ending zero. Next, add "3" from Table 4 to represent "dictionaries." Finally, we find Polish in Table 6 (--91851). An English-Polish dictionary would therefore have this class number: **423.91851**.

42 (Base number for the English language)
+
--3 (Dictionaries from Table 4)
+
--91851 (Polish language from Table 6)
=
423.91851 (English-Polish bilingual dictionary)

Tables 4 and 6 are helpful for building class numbers for language dictionaries, as well as other works that deal with language, such as grammar books and works on etymology, primarily with base numbers originating in the 400s. Table 6 extends our language reach beyond the 400s, as long as we have specific instructions to do so.

TABLE 5

Table 5 (Ethnic and National Groups) allows us to include notation representing ethnic and national groups, if those groups are emphasized in the work you are classifying. This table previously included racial groups as well, but, as of Edition 22, it was removed. Instead, DDC encourages a focus on linguistic and cultural ties (ethnic) and national associations. If we look at the beginning of Table 5, we see an entry for "People of mixed ancestry with ethnic origins from more than one continent" (--05) and an entry for "Europeans and people of European descent" (--09). The --05 notation should be used only when mixed ancestry is emphasized in the work; --09 should be used when a work discusses Europeans and people of European descent more generally, particularly those who identify as "white."

The remainder of Table 5 (--1 through --9) provides notation for specific ethnic and national groups, such as North Americans, Germanic peoples, and Modern Latin people. Like other areas of DDC, --9 provides notation for other ethnic and national groups not listed in notation --1 through --8. All the Table 5 entries can be expanded further if you click on them, so I encourage you to explore what is available in this table. Like with literatures in DDC, Table 5 is Western and Eurocentric. Here is a list of specific ethnic and national groups:

T5--1–T5--9 Specific ethnic and national groups
T5--1 North Americans
T5--2 British, English, Anglo-Saxons
T5--3 Germanic peoples
T5--4 Modern Latin peoples
T5--5 Italians, Romanians, related groups
T5--6 Peoples who speak, or whose ancestors spoke, Spanish, Portuguese, Galician

T5--7 Other Italic peoples
T5--8 Greeks and related groups
T5--9 Other ethnic and national groups

There are multiple ways we can approach the use of Table 5, but I want to focus on what are likely the most common avenues: using instructions found within the schedules or through Table 1 --089 notation. Let's start with the former.

The Use of Table 5 Through Specific Schedule Instructions

A common way to add Table 5 notation is through specific instructions found in the schedule text. Let's use the example of folk music of specific ethnic and national groups (781.62), which (interestingly) represents all "music originating within and associated with an ethnic or national group" (if you try to add ethnicity or national group notation to *popular* music, for example, DDC instructs you to use folk music—oh well!).

First, search for 781.62 and then look at the entry for "Folk music." At 781.621–781.629, which covers "Folk music of specific ethnic and national groups," we are instructed to:

Add to base number 781.62 notation T5--1–T5--9 from Table 5, e.g., Spanish folk music 781.6261.

The Notes area also includes a table that we can use to add further, but let's focus on the basic instruction for now. We are told to start with the base number 781.62, representing folk music of specific ethnic and national groups, and then add to that number notation from Table 5 representing the specific group. In the example provided (Spanish folk music), the Table 5 notation for "People of Spain" (--61) was added to the base number. Let's say we need to classify a book about Celtic folk music. We can browse Table 5 for Celts, or if we are uncertain where to look, we can search for "Celts" using the WebDewey search function and find the entry associated with Table 5 (see Figure 11.2).

Yay—it is the first entry! T5--916. The --916 is located in Table 5 under "Other ethnic and national groups," then under "Other Indo-European peoples." Place --916 after the base number 781.62 to create a class number for Celtic folk music.

Search Results

1.	T5--916	Celts
2.	299.16	Celtic religion
3.	599.981-599.989	Specific ethnic groups with other origins
4.	744.089916	Celts--design
5.	936.4	*Celtic regions to 486
6.	936.4004916	Celts--ancient
7.	941.004916	Celts--modern

Figure 11.2. Search Results for "Celts". *Source*: OCLC

781.62 (Folk music of specific ethnic and national groups)
+
--916 (Celts from Table 5)
=
781.62916 (Celtic folk music)

There are also opportunities to add further notation to the Table 5 notation, either standard subdivisions or geographic places. Let's look at one example at 362.84, which represents social problems of and services to ethnic and national groups.

In the Notes area of 362.841-362.849 - Specific ethnic and national groups, there is an instruction to "Add to base number 362.84 notation T5--1–T5--9 from Table 5, e.g., Italians in United States 362.8451073." The Notes area also emphasizes the need to include notation representing a geographic place, so we need to also consult Table 2. Using the example in WebDewey, we can break down 362.8451073 like so:

362.84 (Social problems of and services to specific ethnic and national groups)
+
--51 (Italians from Table 5)
+
0 (Facet indicator, as instructed at the beginning of Table 5)
+
--73 (United States, from Table 2)
=
362.8451073 (Social problems of and services to Italians in the United States)

Advanced Class Number Building Using Tables 4–6   111

The "facet indicator" of zero mentioned in the example on page 110 is common in DDC numbers built using Table 5. In fact, the third paragraph in the Notes area at the beginning of Table 5 says,

> Except where instructed otherwise, and unless it is redundant, add 0 to the number from this table and to the result add notation T2--1 or T2--3–T2--9 from Table 2 for area in which a group is or was located.

Do your best to follow the instructions and examples provided in the schedule text if you find the Table 5 general instructions to be a bit overwhelming!

The Use of Table 5 Through Table 1 --089

In addition to following instructions found in the schedule text, Table 5 notation can be added via Table 1, specifically using --089 which also represents ethnic and national groups. Whereas the direct application of Table 5 notation can be limited to specific DDC numbers or range of numbers, the use of Table 5 through Table 1 --089 expands our options beyond just what the schedule instructions tell us. Chan and Mitchell state this idea nicely, "The combination of Table 1 and Table 5 notation can be freely added to any class number in the schedules when appropriate."[1]

If we go to --089 within Table 1, we have two main options beyond the standard subdivisions (T1--089001–T1--089009). For "Specific ethnic and national groups with ethnic origins from more than one continent of European descent," we should use the --08905 through --08909 range. Otherwise, use --0891 through --0899 (Specific ethnic and national groups). Choose whichever option makes the most sense for the item you are classifying.

Click on T1--0891–T1--0899 (Specific ethnic and national groups) and we are given the following instructions in the Notes area:

> Add to base number T1--089 notation T5--1-T5--9 from Table 5, e.g., groups of Italian descent T1--08951, groups of Italian descent in United States T1--08951073.

The process the instruction is asking us to follow is very similar to what we have already done except for the addition of --089. As opposed to attaching the Table 5 notation directly onto the main class number, we place --089 in between the main class number and the Table 5 notation. To illustrate this, let's pretend we are classifying a book on stage presentations by modern Greeks. Stage presentations is represented by DDC number 792 and modern Greeks is --893 in Table 5.

792 (Stage presentations)
+
--089 (Ethnic and national groups from Table 1)
+
--893 (Modern Greek people from Table 5)
=
792.089893 (Stage presentations by Modern Greeks)

In conclusion, remember that Tables 4 and 6 provide notation that allows further information about language in a DDC number. Table 4 focuses on the 400 class, but Table 6 provides notation that can be used beyond the 400 class.

You made it through the DDC tables—congratulations! Though clearly not a deep dive into all the DDC tables have to offer, I hope these last few chapters have given you a good foundation on which to continue building your DDC knowledge. Before heading to the last chapter, try the Chapter 11 exercises.

CHAPTER 11 EXERCISES

Answer the following questions using the information provided in this chapter and in WebDewey.
Use Table 4 to construct a class number for each of the following items:

1. A Romanian-language dictionary.
2. A Classical Latin grammar book.
3. A work on the phonology of the Korean language.
4. An introduction to verb phrases in Swedish.

Use Table 6 to construct a class number for each of the following items:

5. A general encyclopedia in Italian.
6. German language instruction in elementary education.
7. Thai folktales.
8. Introduction to the Ojibwa language (a North American native language).

Use Tables 4 and 6 to construct a class number for each of the following items:

9. An English-Classical Greek bilingual dictionary (English is primary).
10. A Japanese-Chinese bilingual dictionary (Japanese is primary).
11. Latin words in the English language.

Use Table 5 to construct a class number for each of the following items:

12. Folk music of the Australian people.
13. Religion of the Ancient Egyptians.
14. Jewish art.
15. Stage presentations of Filipinos.
16. Reading habits of Canadians.

NOTE

1. Chan and Mitchell, *Dewey Decimal Classification*, p. 150.

12

Conclusion and DDC Resources

The end of this book is only the beginning of your DDC journey, so I hope you feel more comfortable finding and assigning DDC numbers than you did when you started this book, even if you don't feel 100 percent confident about everything I covered. As with all cataloging and classification standards, your comfort level usually increases the more you use them, so keep that in mind as you continue to work with DDC. This (final) chapter of the book primarily provides advice and resources for those who need access to DDC and/or more guidance or background on DDC.

Even if you don't look up a DDC number for every item that comes across your desk, it is important to have access to the cataloging tools you need to do your job or complete your homework assignment. As of this writing, an annual subscription to WebDewey is $379.72 for a single-user license in the Americas (https://www.oclc.org/oclc-forms/en/orders/webdewey-order.html). If you or your institution are unable to afford a subscription to WebDewey, it is worth buying a print copy of DDC that can be used as often as you want for many years without having to pay for a subscription (this advice does not apply to students who need access to DDC to complete a course!). The four-volume unabridged set costs $120 per volume, as of this writing (https://www.oclc.org/en/dewey/ordering.html).

In addition to having your tools, if you work in a library, it is important to check your library's catalog to see where your library is placing works on a particular topic. Knowing, for example, that works about the internet in your library are assigned 004.678 can save so much time when another book on the internet comes across your desk. Checking another library's catalog can be a huge help as well. For instance, if you work in a school library, it is helpful to align your classification practices with your local public libraries.

ONLINE RESOURCES

First, some important links for accessing DDC, the introduction, and the summaries:

> Link to sign up for a thirty-day free trial of WebDewey: https://www.oclc.org/content/forms/worldwide/en/webdewey-free-trial.html
> Link to order Dewey Print-On-Demand: https://www.oclc.org/en/dewey/ordering.html
> Introduction to the Dewey Decimal Classification: https://www.oclc.org/content/dam/oclc/dewey/versions/print/intro.pdf
> Summaries (2003):
> https://www.oclc.org/content/dam/oclc/dewey/resources/summaries/deweysummaries.pdf
> Summaries (no date):
> https://www.oclc.org/content/dam/oclc/dewey/ddc23-summaries.pdf

The Melvil Decimal System on **Library Thing**: https://www.librarything.com/mds. Library Thing is primarily known as a social cataloging website similar to Goodreads, but it has also done a ton of work connecting items on the website to DDC numbers. Library Thing created the Melvil Decimal System using not the copyrighted DDC, but (according to the website) "the classification work of libraries around the world, whose assignments are not copyrightable." Therefore, you can go to the Melvil Decimal System website and click on the desired class, division, and section number (and beyond!) to see the topics associated with each, as well as the books in Library Thing associated with the topic. The interface color-codes the numbers and levels and is quite fun to play with!

BOOKS

Chan, L. M., and Mitchell, J. S. (2003). *Dewey Decimal Classification: Principles and application.* Third edition. OCLC.
   Though focused on the 22nd edition of DDC, Chan and Mitchell's text is still a fantastic guide to understanding current versions of DDC. It also contains exercises for most chapters. Chan and Mitchell are both respected experts on DDC; Mitchell was also a DDC editor in chief.

Comaromi, J. P. (1976). *The Eighteen Editions of the Dewey Decimal Classification.* Albany, NY: Forest Press.
   For those interested in learning more about the history of DDC, Comaromi, a DDC scholar and former DDC editor in chief, is an excellent guide. This fascinating book provides a comprehensive history of DDC up until the 18th edition published in 1971.

Farkas, L. (2015). *Learn Dewey Decimal Classification (Edition 23).* International edition. TotalRecall Publications.
   Farkas's book on DDC focuses on the 23rd edition and is more of a workbook; it lacks the in-depth discussion of DDC present in Chan and Mitchell. If you are looking for more practice, you have found the right book!

Kyrios, A., and Satija, M. P. (2023). *A Handbook of History, Theory and Practice of the Dewey Decimal Classification System.* Facet Publishing.
   This is the most recent text on DDC (other than the one you are reading right now, of course!) written by DDC scholar M. P. Satija and DDC editor Alex Kyrios. Though lacking in exercises, this authoritative text provides great in-depth discussion of all aspects of DDC. I recommend this book especially to those who need to take full advantage of DDC number building.

Wiegand, W. A. (1996). *Irrepressible Reformer: A Biography of Melvil Dewey.* American Library Association.
   If you want to learn more about the creator of DDC, Melvil Dewey, Wiegand's book is a great source. Wiegand spends very little time on DDC in this book because, as you will see if you read it, Dewey was involved in so many things beyond DDC that it makes your head spin!

DDC COURSES/LEARNING RESOURCES

There are various resources out there if you are interested in learning DDC in a more structured environment. On occasion, the Core division of the American Library Association offers an online course on DDC through its Fundamentals series (https://www.ala.org/core/continuing-education/courses), so check that website regularly in addition to the following:

Dewey Training Courses: https://www.oclc.org/en/dewey/resources/teachingsite.html. This freely available resource from OCLC is, according to the website, "an online set of training materials for the DDC focused on the needs of experienced librarians who need Dewey application training." OCLC provides slides on various DDC and WebDewey topics, along with exercises to test your learning. Much of the material is, admittedly, a bit dated, with most slides and exercises containing dates from 2012 or 2013. Nonetheless, this resource provides good supplemental information and exercises if you need to dig deeper into DDC topics than what I covered in this book.

Library Juice Academy course on Dewey Decimal Classification: https://libraryjuiceacademy.com/. If you prefer a learning environment guided by a real instructor and fellow classmates to engage with, consider this online course from Library Juice Academy. LJA offers a four-week, hands-on, asynchronous course on DDC that, as of this writing, costs $200.

WebJunction course Shelving with Dewey: https://www.webjunction.org/news/webjunction/dewey-course-updated.html. This self-paced course by WebJunction introduces DDC so future shelvers understand the logic behind it. Shelving simulations are included as well! You must create an account with WebJunction, but the course is free.

Appendix A: Answers to End-of-Chapter Exercises

CHAPTER 1: DEWEY DECIMAL CLASSIFICATION IN A NUTSHELL

1. What two things does DDC allow us to do with library collections? **It allows us to both categorize and provide a way to locate a resource within library collections.**
2. In which DDC class do we assign works on library science? **000**
3. Which class number was originally titled the "Useful Arts"? **600**
4. True or False—The index to DDC is called Melvil's Awesome Index. **It would be pretty funny if this were true, but alas, it is False. The index to the DDC is called the Relative Index.**
5. What does it mean to say that a classification system is "expressive"? Provide an example that shows expressive notation. **"Expressive" in this context means that the symbols used to represent a topic also express the hierarchical relationship it has to other topics. An example of expressive notation used in this chapter is 616, which represents Diseases, within Medicine & health (610), within Technology (600).**
6. In the DDC number 306, which number represents the DDC . . .
Section? **6. The third digit of the class number represents the section**
Main Class? **3. The first digit of the class number represents the main class**

Division? **0. The second digit of the class number represents the division**
7. True or False—DDC numbers will always be at least three digits long. **True**
8. Who publishes DDC? Is DDC still published in print? **OCLC currently publishes DDC, and it is published print-on-demand only.**
9. In the DDC schedules, what do we call the term that provides the specific meaning of a notation? **The caption, sometimes called the heading, provides the specific meaning of a notation in the DDC schedules. For example, "Diseases" is the caption for 616.**
10. True or False—A DDC number with a decimal point can end with a zero. **False. There are DDC numbers that end with a zero. However, DDC numbers containing a decimal point should never end with a zero.**

CHAPTER 2: BASIC PRINCIPLES OF CLASSIFICATION

1. I am cataloging a book about pancakes (641.8153) and biscuits (641.8157), which are discussed equally in the book. Under which DDC number should I class this book and why? **641.8153—First-of-two rule. Since both topics are treated equally in the book, choose the class number that comes first in the schedules, which is 641.8153 (pancakes).**
2. I am cataloging a book about the architecture of metal roofs. I could classify this book under 721.0447 (the use of metals as architectural material) or 721.5 (the architecture of roofs and roof structures). Under which DDC number should I class this book and why? **721.5—Rule of zero. If both class numbers are equally good to use, prefer the one with fewer zeroes and a fourth digit that is not a zero.**
3. I am cataloging a book about the interior decoration of day care centers. I could classify this book under interior decoration (747) or day care centers (362.712). Under which DDC number should I class this book and why? **362.712—Table of last resort. Day care centers are "kinds of things," higher up in the table of prefer-**

Appendix A: Answers to End-of-Chapter Exercises 121

ence than interior decoration, which would be an "operation upon things, parts, or materials." The First-of-two rule is also a possibility here but does not fit as well since these topics are used to introduce or explain one another.

4. I am cataloging a book that discusses equally the topics of surfing (797.32), water skiing (797.35), and jet skiing (797.37), which are all under the broader topic of "Other aquatic sports" (797.3). Under which DDC number should I class this book and why? **797.3—Rule of three. Since all three topics are discussed equally, the rule of three says to choose the first higher class number that includes all the subjects.**
5. I am cataloging a book about the ethics of vice (179.8) and virtue (179.9), but the author focuses more on vice than virtue. Under which DDC number should I class this book and why? **179.8—Fuller treatment. Since vice is discussed more the virtue, choose vice (179.8).**
6. I am cataloging a book on the effects of postpartum depression (618.76) on working mothers (331.44). Under which DDC number should I class this book and why? **331.44—Rule of application. Postpartum depression is acting upon the working mothers, so the rule of application tells us that we should choose the class number that is being acted upon (331.44—working mothers).**

CHAPTER 3: WEBDEWEY: THE ONLINE PORTAL TO DDC

1. Which WebDewey feature allows you to bring up a list of changes to DDC within the last thirty days? **Updates**
2. Is there a way to add comments to class numbers in WebDewey? **Yes, through the Comments feature**.
3. How many tables are in the abridged DDC15? **4**
4. True or False—There is a Dewey Blog maintained by Dewey editors. **True**
5. If I don't currently have access to WebDewey, is there a way for me to try it out for free? **Yes. OCLC offers a thirty-day trial of WebDewey during which you can access it for free.**

6. Go to the glossary and find the entry for "scope note." How does DDC define "scope note"? **Scope note: A note indicating that the meaning of a class number is broader or narrower than is apparent from the heading.**
7. From the WebDewey home page, click on the Technology class (600) and find the class number for Chemical Engineering. What is that class number? **660**
8. What is the class number for Food technology within Chemical Engineering, within the Technology class? **664**
9. From the WebDewey home page, browse the main DDC numbers, divisions, and possibly sections to find the topics the following class numbers represent:
   a. 210 **Philosophy & theory of religion (within Religion)**
   b. 328 **The legislative process (within Political science)**
   c. 750 **Painting (within Arts & recreation)**
   d. 913 **Geography of and travel in the ancient world (within Geography & travel)**
   e. 093 **Incunabula (within Manuscripts & rare books)**
   f. 549 **Mineralogy (within Chemistry)**
   g. 498 **South American native languages (within Other languages)**

CHAPTER 4: SEARCHING AND BROWSING IN WEBDEWEY

1. What is a "built number" in WebDewey? **Built numbers are created using a number from the DDC schedules and other notation, usually from one (or more) of the DDC tables.**
2. True or False—The Relative Index retrieves entries in alphabetical order? **True**
3. True or False—"Browse" and "Search" results are interchangeable and produce the same results. **False. "Search" results will be listed numerically ascending by DDC number and will be pulled from all areas of the schedules. "Browse" results will present captions in alphabetical order from the Relative Index.**
4. True or False—"Notes" can be ignored when using WebDewey. **False. Please do not ignore the Notes!**

Appendix A: Answers to End-of-Chapter Exercises 123

5. How is the "Link to OPAC" at the top of the page handy and what can it be used for? **The "Link to OPAC" button is preprogrammed to take you to the Library of Congress' catalog listing of all works in their collection that are assigned the class number. This feature is particularly handy if you want to confirm the types of resources to which a class number is typically assigned.**

Searching WebDewey

Find the DDC number that best fits the following topics.

6. Neanderthals **569.986**
7. Proverbs (not biblical) from around the world **398.9**
8. World War I **940.3**
9. Judaism **296**
10. Loch Ness monster **001.944**

Browsing DDC numbers

Find the general topic associated with the following DDC numbers.

11. 133.12 **Haunted places**
12. 331.892 **Strikes (specifically labor strikes)**
13. 814 **American essays in English**
14. 025.431 **Dewey Decimal Classification**
15. 413.17 **Picture dictionaries**

Use WebDewey's Search and Browse to find an appropriate DDC number for nonfiction books with the following titles:

16. *Feng Shui for Small Spaces: An Introduction to Geomancy.* **133.3337**
17. *Go Scuba Diving!* **797.234**
18. *The History of the Ancient World: From the Earliest Accounts to the Fall of Rome.* **930**
19. *Crystallography for Beginners.* **548**
20. *Scholarships in Higher Education.* **378.34**

21. *The Story of Juneteenth.* **394.263. Though most commonly placed in holidays, nonfiction books about Juneteenth are sometimes placed in history instead, specifically within Texas history.**

CHAPTER 5: USING NOTES AND THE MANUAL

1. At 736.4 (Wood carving), the Note area says that what topics are also included at this class number? **"butter prints and molds, whittling"**
2. What kind of haunted places are included at 133.122? Also, what do I do if I am classifying a specific haunted place? **The specific types of haunted places are "haunted churches, forests, graveyards, houses." "Class specific haunted places regardless of type in 133.129."**
3. What DDC number should I assign to a work titled *Guide to Chamber Music*? **785, which says to "Class here chamber music."**
4. Go to 364 (Criminology) and review the table of preference in the Note area for that class number. Answer the following two questions using that table of preference:
   a. According to the table of preference, should I class a work on the causes of specific types of criminal offenses in 364.1 or in 364.2? **364.2 (Causes of crime and delinquency is higher in the table of preference than criminal offenses).**
   b. According to the table of preference, where should I class a work on the history of discharged offenders? **364.8 (Discharged offenders, which is higher in the table of preference than History, geographic treatment, biography).**
5. Find the Manual entry for 551.5 versus 551.6 (Meteorology versus Climatology and weather) and answer the following questions:
   a. What class number should I choose if I am classifying a book titled *Climate and Weather* that also covers topics in meteorology? **551.5—The Manual says to use 551.5 for works called "climatology," "climate and weather," or simply "climate" or "weather," if they cover topics in meteorology.**
   b. I need to classify a book about microclimatology. Should I choose 551.5 or 551.6? **551.6—even more specifically 551.66**

c. After reading through the 551.5 vs. 551.6 entry in the Manual, I am still uncertain about which class number to choose. If I am in doubt, which class number should I choose? **551.5**
6. Find the Manual entry for 004.678 versus 006.7, 025.042, 384.33 (Internet and World Wide Web) and answer the following questions:
   a. Which class number should I choose if the book I am classifying is about web page design? **006.7**
   b. I have a book that is about the internet and World Wide Web that focuses more on information science than computer science. Should I class this work in 004.678 or 025.042? **025.042—the Manual entry says, "Interdisciplinary works about the Internet and WWW that do not contain enough computer science material to be classified in 004.678, but that do contain some information science material" should be classed in 025.042.**
   c. True or False—If I am in doubt about which class number to choose, I should prefer 006.7. **False. I should prefer 004.678. The Manual says, "If in doubt, prefer in the following order: 004.678, 025.042, 006.7, 384.33."**

CHAPTER 6: NUMBER BUILDING IN DDC USING A FULL OR PART OF A NUMBER FROM THE SCHEDULES

Exercises with Number Building by Adding a Full Number

1. Use the instruction at 418.03 (Translating materials on specific subjects) to create class numbers for the following topics:
   a. Translating materials on Aristotelian philosophy **418.03185– 418.03 (Translating materials on specific subjects) + 185 (Aristotelian philosophy).**
   b. Translating materials on astronomy (generally, within Science) **418.0352–418.03 (Translating materials on specific subjects) + 52 (Astronomy, within Science–exclude final zero).**
   c. Translating materials on the passage of legislation **418.03328375– 418.03 (Translating materials on specific subjects) + 328375 (Passing of legislation—328.375).**

2. Use the instruction at 659.19001–659.19999 (subdivisions for specific kinds of organizations, products, services within Advertising) to create class numbers for the following topics:
    a. Advertising jewelry. **659.193917–659.19 (Advertising for specific kinds of organizations, products, services) + 391.7 (Jewelry, exclude decimal point).**
    b. Advertising statistical software. **659.1900555–659.19 (Advertising for specific kinds of organizations, products, services) + 005.55 (Statistical software, exclude decimal point).**
    c. Advertising pet food. **659.1966466–659.19 (Advertising for specific kinds of organizations, products, services) + 664.66 (Food for animals, exclude decimal point).**

Exercises with Number Building by Adding Part of a Number

3. Use the instructions at 205.6 (Specific moral issues, sins, vices, virtues) to create class numbers for the following topics:
    a. Morality of the consumption of alcoholic beverages **205.681–205.6 (Specific moral issues, sins, vices, virtues) + 81 (from 178.1—Consumption of alcoholic beverages).**
    b. Morality of the gambling business **205.646–205.6 (Specific moral issues, sins, vices, virtues) + 46 (from 174.6—Gambling business).**
    c. Morality of nuclear weapons and nuclear war **205.62422–205.6 (Specific moral issues, sins, vices, virtues) + 2422 (from 172.422—Nuclear weapons and nuclear war; this one is buried under International relations—War and peace).**
4. Use the instructions at 641.63–641.67 (Cooking food derived from plant crops and domesticated animals) to create class numbers for the following topics:
    a. Cooking with grapes **641.648–641.6 (Cooking food derived from plant crops and domesticated animals) + 48 (from 634.8—Grapes).**
    b. Cooking with kola nuts **641.6376–641.6 (Cooking food derived from plant crops and domesticated animals) + 376 (from 633.76—Kola nuts [Cola nuts]).**

Appendix A: Answers to End-of-Chapter Exercises 127

c. Cooking with turkey **641.66592–641.6 (Cooking food derived from plant crops and domesticated animals) + 6592 (from 636.592—Turkeys)**.

Exercises with More Complex Number Building

5. Use the instruction at 387.21–387.29 (Specific types of ships) to create class numbers for the following topics:
   a. Hand-propelled and towed craft **387.29–387.2 (Specific types of ships) + 9 (from 623.829—Hand-propelled and towed craft).
   By the way, the class numbers at 623.821–623.829 relate to the engineering of the specified ship, not to the type of ship generally, in case you were wondering about the difference between 387.2 and 623.82. See 629.046 vs. 388 (Transportation equipment vs. Transportation) within the Manual.**
   b. Ferryboats **387.234–387.2 (Specific types of ships) + 34 (from 623.8234—Ferryboats).**
   c. Warships **387.225–387.2 (Specific types of ships) + 25 (from 623.8225—Warships).**

CHAPTER 7: ADVANCED CLASS NUMBER BUILDING USING TABLE 1—PART 1—THE BASICS OF ADDING STANDARD SUBDIVISIONS

1. True or False—Table notations can be used alone. **False. Never use a table notation alone.**
2. True or False—It is okay to leave off the standard subdivision to save time and/or spine label space. **True. Standard subdivisions are helpful, but not required.**

Find the Table 1 notation that represents the following topics:

3. Philosophy and theory **--01**
4. Management of materials **--0687**
5. Patents and identification marks **--027**
6. Statistical methods **--0727**

For each of the following topics, find the appropriate class number and Table 1 notation:

7. An encyclopedia of zodiac signs. **133.5203—zodiac signs (133.52) + encyclopedias (--03)**
8. A work on the classification of commercially produced beer and ale. **663.42012—commercially produced beer and ale (663.42) + classification (--012)**
9. Historical research on public libraries. **027.40722—public libraries (027.4) + historical research (--0722)**
10. A work on psychology as a profession. **150.23—since psychology 150 ends with a zero, do not include the additional zero unless instructed otherwise—150 (psychology) + as a profession (--23)**
11. A humorous treatment of horses (from the animal husbandry perspective). **636.100207—include an additional zero to avoid a conflict with the special topics in the husbandry of horses (636.101–636.108) – horses (636.1) + humorous treatment (--00207)**

Deconstruct the meaning of each DDC number below. Each contains a class number and a Table 1 notation.

12. 300.71. **Social sciences education**
13. 211.012. **Classification of concepts of God**
14. 795.403. **A dictionary, encyclopedia, or concordance on card games**

CHAPTER 8: ADVANCED CLASS NUMBER BUILDING USING TABLE 1—PART 2—APPROXIMATING THE WHOLE, GROUPS OF PEOPLE, BIOGRAPHY, AND HISTORICAL PERIODS

1. True or False—I can add a standard subdivision to DDC 357 (Mounted forces and warfare). **True. Dual headings approximate the whole of the class number. Plus, the Notes area for 357 says, "Standard subdivisions are added for either or both topics in heading."**

Appendix A: Answers to End-of-Chapter Exercises 129

2. True or False—I can add a standard subdivision to DDC 667.3 (Dyeing and printing) for works about printing alone. **False. Number 667.3, which represents dyeing and printing within chemical engineering, has in its Notes area, "Standard subdivisions are added for dyeing and printing together, for dyeing alone." Therefore, standard subdivisions cannot be added to works about printing alone—only to works about dyeing along, or printing and dyeing together.**
3. True or False—I can add a standard subdivision to DDC 776 (Computer art (Digital art)) if I assign this class number to a work about artistic aspects of virtual reality. **False. At 776, there is a note that says, "Including artistic aspects of virtual reality." Topics in "Including" notes do not approximate the whole of the class and should not be assigned a standard subdivision, if that applies. If "artistic aspects of virtual reality" was in a "Class here" note, that would mean that it approximates the whole of the class.**

Find the notation in Table 1 (T1--0901–T1--0905) for the following historical periods:

4. 2000–2019 --**09051**
5. 16th century, 1500–1599 --**09031**
6. 999–1 BCE --**09014**
7. Middle Ages (Medieval period) --**0902 (see Notes area)**

Create a DDC number for the following topics using Table 1 notation (underlined in the descriptions below) and explain how you arrived at that number:

8. A book containing <u>research</u> on the manufacture of blouses. **687.115072. First, make sure you choose 687.115, which represents the <u>manufacture</u> of shirts, blouses, and tops (there are other class numbers that include blouses, but not specifically related to manufacturing). "Research" is represented by the Table 1 notation --072. Since we are instructed at 687.115 that "Standard subdivisions are added for any or all topics in heading," we are safe to put --072 after 687.115 for blouse manufacturing only.**

9. An encyclopedia of Atlantis. **001.94 (Mysteries),** Including Atlantis, Bermuda Triangle, pyramid power. Atlantis does not approximate the whole of "Mysteries" so do not add Table 1 notation for encyclopedias.
10. A serial publication on social psychoanalysis education. **302.17071.** Social psychoanalysis is represented by 302.17 (Social dysfunction). We can add Table 1 notation to this class number because social psychoanalysis does approximate the whole of social dysfunction (social psychoanalysis is in a "class here" note). However, there are two potential Table 1 notations we could include: serial publication (--05) or education (--071). We cannot include both, so look at the Table of Preference at the beginning of Table 1. Education is higher in the Table of Preference than serial publications, so we include only --071 (education) at the end of 302.17.
11. Money-saving cooking for married people. **641.55208655.** Money-saving cooking is at 641.552. "Married people" is part of the Groups of People area (--08) of Table 1, specifically --08655 (drill down into "People by miscellaneous social attributes" and then "People by marital status). There are no instructions otherwise, so it is fine to simply place --08655 at the end of 641.552.
12. A biography of a mathematician. **510.92.** First, find the class number for mathematics (510), and then add Table 1 notation for biography (--092). Since 510 ends with a zero, drop the zero before adding the table notation.
13. Ancient board games for fun and amusement. **794.0901.** Board games are classed at 794. Then add the "ancient" aspect, use Table 1—Historical periods (T1--0901–T1--0905). The "ancient period" not confined to a specific geographic area is represented by --0901 (To 499 CE).

Deconstruct these DDC numbers by explaining the class number, standard subdivision, and/or special notation.

14. 681.114092. **This class number represents a biography of a watchmaker. Start with the DDC number for watches (681.114) and then the Table 1 notation --092 represents biography.**

15. 791.4509048. **This class number represents works about 1980s television shows. 791.45 represents televisions shows, and --09048 from Table 1 represents the 1980s.**
16. 641.56110904. **This class number represents works about cooking for one in the 20th century. 641.5611 represents cooking for one, and --0904 from Table 1 represents the 20th century.**

CHAPTER 9: ADVANCED CLASS NUMBER BUILDING—INCLUDING GEOGRAPHIC PLACES USING TABLE 2

1. True or False—Geography can only be noted by using Table 2. **False. Geographic information can be included in other ways, notably incorporated into existing class numbers in certain areas of the DDC schedules.**
2. True or False—Table 2 allows you to include notation representing socioeconomic regions by political orientation. **True. See Table 2 --171.**
3. True or False. I suggest using any and all tables and special notations that you can to create the longest possible call number. **False. Please don't do this! Follow DDC instructions for adding table and special notations, which don't allow you to add as many notations as you want.**

Find the Table 2 notation for the following geographic places, either by browsing Table 2 or using the Relative Index:

4. Algeria **--65**
5. South Georgia and South Sandwich Islands **--9712**
6. The planet Jupiter **--9925**
7. Iceland **--4912**
8. Southern Hemisphere **--1814**

Create a DDC number for the following works using either Table 2 or a combination of Table 1 and Table 2.

9. A book on cooking brunch in the United States. **641.520973**
   641.52 (Brunch within Cooking) + --09 (from Table 1) + --73 (United States from Table 2)
10. A travel guidebook for Brazil. **918.104**
    91 (Base notation for geography and travel) + --81 (Brazil from Table 2) + --04 (Notation for travel guidebooks, from the table at 913-919)
11. A history of Ancient Greece during the Hellenistic period, 323–146 BCE. **938.08**
    For this one, Table 2 is not needed. Simply go to DDC number 930 (History of ancient world (to ca. 499)) and drill down to "Specific places" then "Greece to 323" and "Hellenistic period, 323–146 B.C." is an option within Greece. Since this is within the history class, we do not need to add further Table 1 notation for history as that would be redundant. However, 938 is technically a "built number" using Table 2, with "9" representing history, and --38 from Table 2.
12. A book on sports in Central America **796.09728**
    796 (Sports) + --09 (from Table 1) + --728 (Central America from Table 2)
13. A book on the geography of Southeast Asia. **915.9**
    91 (base number from instructions at 913-919) + --59 (Southeast Asia from Table 2). No need to include the --09 from Table 1 because of the instructions at 913–919.
14. A book on printmaking in the Mariana Islands. **769.9967**
    769.9 (base number from 769.91–769.99) + --967 (Mariana Islands from Table 2). The instruction at 769.91–769.99 (Printmaking and Prints—Geographic treatment, biography) says to add to base number 769.9 notation from Table 2.

CHAPTER 10: ADVANCED CLASS NUMBER BUILDING USING TABLE 3—SUBDIVISIONS FOR THE ARTS, FOR INDIVIDUAL LITERATURES, FOR SPECIFIC LITERARY FORMS

1. According to Table 3A, which notation represents Fiction? What about Miscellaneous writings? **Fiction is represented by --3 in Table 3A and Miscellaneous writing is represented by --8.**

2. According to Table 3B, which notation represents Humor and satire? What about Diaries, journals, notebooks, reminiscences? **Humor and satire are represented by --7 in Table 3B and Diaries, journals, notebooks, reminiscences are represented by --803.**
3. According to Table 3C, which notation represents literature displaying stream of consciousness? What about Arts and literature dealing with plants? **Stream of consciousness is represented by --25 in Table 3C and Arts and literature dealing with plants is represented by --364.**

Use Table 3A to create a class number for the following works:

4. The novel *Frankenstein*, by English author Mary Shelley (1797–1851). **823.7**
5. *If It Bleeds*, a collection of short stories by American author Stephen King (1947–). **813.54 (even though King is still a prolific author today, his works are classed largely in the 1945-1999 time period (--54) because that is when he started his writing career)**
6. *Mord auf Raten*, a novel by German author Andreas Franz (1954–2011). **833.92 (German fiction is 833 and most of Franz's novels have been published since 1990 (--92 on the period table)).**
7. *Bad Feminist*, a book of essays by American author Roxane Gay (1974–). **814.6**
8. *Call Us What We Carry*, a book of poems by American poet Amanda Gorman (1998–). **811.6**
9. A collection of plays by Irish playwright, poet, and author Oscar Wilde (1854–1900). **822.8**

Use Tables 3B (and potentially Table 3C) to a create a class number for the following works:

10. A collection of essays by Spanish authors. **864**
11. An anthology of English ghost stories. **823.08733**
    (823 = English fiction and --08733 from Table 3B—Specific Kinds of Fiction)
12. A collection of English ballads from the Queen Anne period. **821.0440805**

(821.044 = English ballads from 800 class and T3B--102–T3B--107 [Specific kinds of poetry], then add –080 for specific periods, and --5 for the Queen Anne period on the period table)
13. An anthology of French drama for children. **842.089282**
(84 [French literature] + --2 [Drama from Table 3B] + --08 [Notation from Table 3B] +--9282 [Children from Table 3C]) Remember: even though T3B--2 Drama doesn't provide explicit guidance, you must recall Step 3 from the Notes at Table 3B that indicate the use of T3B--102-T3B--107 for specific forms for which subdivisions are added. This may seem counterintuitive as T3B--1 resides under Poetry but it is used with for all forms that meet at least one of the criteria listed in Step 3.
14. An American collection of humor and satire that has a "holiday" theme. **817.08334**
(81 [American literature] + --7 [Humor & Satire from Table 3B] + --08 [Notation from Table 3B] +--334 [Holidays from Table 3C])

Use Table 3C to create a class number for the following works:

15. Electronic games featuring animals. **794.8462 (794.84 (Specific aspects of electronic games) + --62 (Animals from Table 3C, the numbers following --3, as instructed)**
16. A collection of literature that features magic and witchcraft. **808.80377 (808.80 [Base number for collections of literature displaying specific features—808.801–808.803] + --377 [Magic and witchcraft from Table 3C])**
17. A work on nontraditional viewpoints in the arts. **700.411 (700.41 [Base number for arts displaying specific qualities of style, mood, viewpoint] + --1 [Nontraditional viewpoints from Table 3C, one "1" removed based upon instruction at 700.41]).**

Appendix A: Answers to End-of-Chapter Exercises 135

CHAPTER 11: ADVANCED CLASS NUMBER BUILDING USING TABLES 4–6—LANGUAGES AND ETHNIC & NATIONAL GROUPS

Use Table 4 to construct a class number for each of the following items:

1. A Romanian-language dictionary. **459.3 (Romanian language [459] + --3 from Table 4)**
2. A Classical Latin grammar book. **475 (Classical Latin [47] + --5 from Table 4)**
3. A work on the phonology of the Korean language. **495.715 (Korean [495.7] + --15 from Table 4)**
4. An introduction to verb phrases in Swedish. **439.756 (Swedish [439.7] + --56 from Table 4)**

Use Table 6 to construct a class number for each of the following items:

5. A general encyclopedia in Italian. **036.51 (General encyclopedias [036] + --51 [Italian] from Table 6)**
6. German language instruction in elementary education. **372.6531 (Second languages in elementary education [372.65] + --31 [German from Table 6])**
7. Thai folktales. **398.20495911 (Folk literature by language [398.204] + --95911 [Thai from Table 6])**
8. Introduction to the Ojibwa language (a North American native language). **497.333 (Algic and Muskogean languages [497.3] + --33 [Ojibwa from Table 6]). Follow the instructions in the Notes area of 497.3.**

Use Tables 4 and 6 to construct a class number for each of the following items:

9. An English-Classical Greek bilingual dictionary (English is primary). **423.81 (English language [42] + --3 [Dictionaries from Table 4] + --81 [Classical Greek from Table 6])**
10. A Japanese-Chinese bilingual dictionary (Japanese is primary). **495.63951 (Japanese language [495.6] + --3 [Dictionaries from Table 4] + --951 [Chinese from Table 6])**

11. Latin words in the English language. **422.471 (English language [42] + --24 [Elements from foreign languages in Table 4] + --71 [Latin from Table 6])**

Use Table 5 to construct a class number for each of the following items:

12. Folk music of the Australian people. **781.6224 (Folk music of specific ethnic and national groups [781.62] + --24 [Australians from Table 5])**
13. Religion of the Ancient Egyptians. **299.31 (Religions not provided for elsewhere [299] + --31 [Ancient Egyptians from Table 5]). See instruction in the Notes area of 299.1–299.4.**
14. Jewish art. **704.03924 (Ethnic and national groups within Special topics in fine and decorative arts [704.03] + --924 [Hebrews, Israelis, Jews from Table 5]).**

    Use the Notes area instruction at 704.031–704.039 (Specific ethnic and national groups) to build this class number.
15. Stage presentations of Filipinos. **792.0899921 (Stage presentations [792] + --089 [Ethnic and national groups from Table 1] + --9921 [Filipinos from Table 5]).**
16. Reading habits of Canadians. **028.908911 (Reading habits [028.9] + --089 [Ethnic and national groups from Table 1] + --11 [Canadians from Table 5]).**

Appendix B: Flow Chart for Works By or About More Than One Author

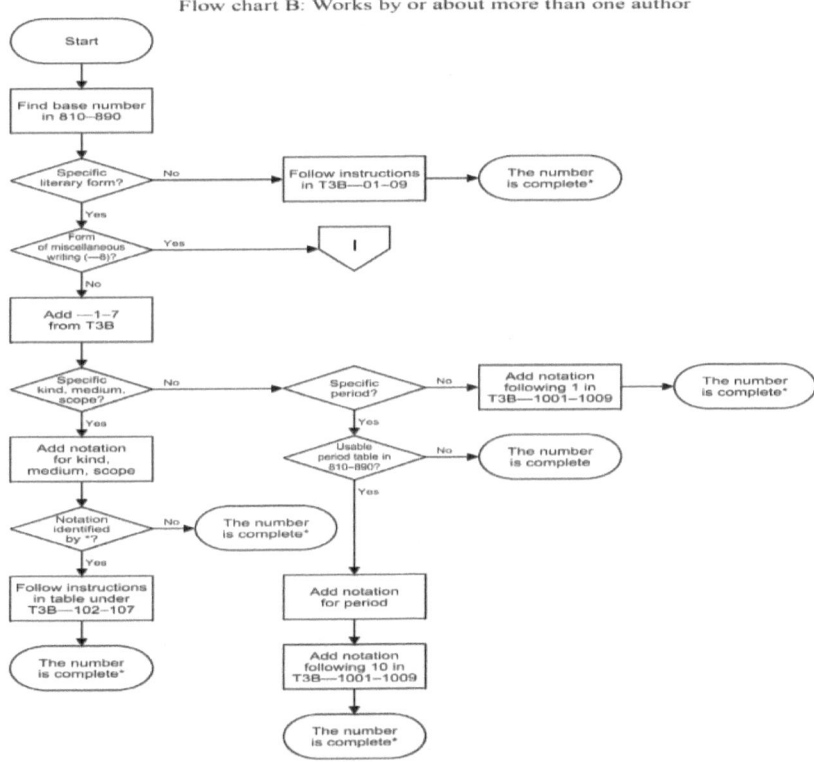

Flow chart B: Works by or about more than one author

*If appropriate, standard subdivisions may be added

https://www.oclc.org/content/dam/oclc/webdewey/help/full_manual.pdf

Glossary

The following Glossary contains terms I bolded throughout this book, along with their definitions. I recommend referring to the Dewey Decimal Classification (DDC) glossary provided by OCLC as well: https://help.oclc.org/Librarian_Toolbox/OCLC_glossaries/Dewey_Decimal_Classification_glossary.

Approximating the whole—the idea that the class number you choose should align as closely as possible to the subject of the work you are cataloging. You may add a standard subdivision to any class number that approximates the whole of the subject or discipline, unless instructed otherwise.

Built number—DDC numbers that are composed of a base class number and other notation, usually from one (or more) of the DDC tables. The orange puzzle piece next to DDC numbers in WebDewey indicates the class number is a built number.

Call number—notation, of which the classification number is a part, that is assigned to each resource to provide its "address" in relation to other resources that have the same or a similar topic. Call numbers can also contain notation that brings together works by or about an individual author, or by literary form or genre.

Caption—also called a heading, a caption is the term that presents the specific meaning of the notation in English words (for example, "Diseases" is the caption for the class number 616).

Expressive notation—notation that communicates the hierarchical relationships of the topic it represents.

Heading—see Caption.

Hierarchical classification system—a system of organization in which broader topics are subdivided into narrower topics within a specific category.

Manual—a guide to the DDC that pays particular attention to challenges that arise when assigning DDC numbers and provides guidance when multiple DDC numbers seem applicable.

Notation—within DDC, notation is a series of Arabic numbers that represent a specific topic, either representing a class, division, and subdivision (and at least three digits long), or representing topics, forms, time periods and more from the DDC tables.

Relative Index—the index to the DDC that brings together all locations of a subject under one entry. It lists subjects alphabetically, and then alphabetically by discipline within each subject.

Schedules—the list of concepts within a classification system, organized by classification number, that includes the notations, captions, and instructions for the class numbers.

Standard subdivisions—notations from Table 1 that supplement the main topic of a work and "represent frequently recurring physical forms (dictionaries, periodicals) or approaches (history, research) applicable to any subject or discipline."[1]

WebDewey—the online, subscription-based portal to DDC that provides access to not only the DDC schedules and tables, but also other features and helpful documents..

NOTE

1. Chan and Mitchell, *Dewey Decimal Classification*, p. 81.

Index

approximating the whole, 56, 59–60, 139
author numbers. *See* Cutter numbers.

book numbers. *See* Cutter numbers.
built number, 28, 31, 139

call number, x, 139
caption, 8, 139
Cutter numbers, 9–10, 90–91

Dewey, Melvil, ix–xi, 3–4, 118
division of DDC number, 6, 54

expressive notation, 5–6, 139

first-of-two rule, 16
fuller treatment rule, 16, 18
fixed location system, ix

genre, 5, 87, 91, 93–94

heading. *See* caption
hierarchical classification system, 5–6, 139

LCSH. *See* Library of Congress Subject Headings
Library of Congress Subject Headings (LCSH), 31

Machine-Readable Cataloging (MARC), 32
main class of DDC number, 6, 23, 54
the Manual, xi, 24, 36–37, 63–65, 80, 91, 139
MARC. *See* Machine–Readable Cataloging

notation, 1, 5–8, 139
notes, xi, 31–32, 35–39

Relative Index, 8, 29, 31, 44, 139
relative location system, x
rule of application, 16
rule of three, 17
rule of zero, 17–18

schedules, 8–9, 16–17, 21, 28–29, 31, 41, 50–53, 55, 73, 75, 79, 82, 88, 104–106, 109, 139

section of DDC number, 6
special notation, 57n1, 59–60, 66–70, 81–82
standard subdivisions, 49–56, 59–61, 68, 82, 92, 105, 110–111, 139

Table 1, 7–8, 41, 49–56, 86
Table 2, 7, 39, 50, 70, 73–82
Table 3, 14, 49–50, 64, 82, 85–100; Table 3A, 85–92, 100; Table 3B, 85–86, 91–100 Table 3C, 85–86, 95–100

Table 4, 50, 103–108, 112
Table 5, 50, 103, 108–112
Table 6, 50, 103–108, 112
table of last resort, 18
table of preference, 37–39, 59–62, 66–69, 81, 88, 93

WebDewey, x–xi, 9, 19, 21–24, 27–32, 36, 42, 50, 52, 61, 87, 109–110, 115–116, 118, 139

About the Author

Karen Snow is a professor in the School of Information Studies at Dominican University in River Forest, Illinois. She teaches face-to-face and online in the areas of cataloging, classification, and metadata. Her main areas of research interest are cataloging quality, ethics, and education. In addition to numerous journal articles and book chapters, she has published two books with Rowman & Littlefield—*A Practical Guide to Library of Congress Classification* (2017) and *A Practical Guide to Library of Congress Subject Headings* (2021)—and coauthored the *Core Competencies for Cataloging and Metadata Professional Librarians* (2017) and the *Cataloguing Code of Ethics* (2021).

www.ingramcontent.com/pod-product-compliance
Lightning Source LLC
Chambersburg PA
CBHW030141240426
43672CB00005B/223